ENCOUNTERS
OF THE GOD-KIND

By M. Sue Alexander

First Edition, CrossBooks
2011, USA

Second Edition, Suzander Publishing, LLC
2015, USA

Copyright © 2011 by M. Sue Alexander

Cover Design by Kara Suzanne Leist

Novel Series by Author

Resurrection Dawn 2014
Christian Fiction Series

Victoria Tempest wakes up from twenty-five-years of amnesia and doesn't recognize her surroundings. The night she wrecked her car in 1989 her attorney-husband was murdered. On a quest to solve the mystery, she encounters many obstacles as a Christian.

E-Books Only

The Forum

In a near-death experience, stock-broker Jacob Barker is catapulted to a place called *The Forum*. What he spiritually believes determines which door he will next enter. After being revived, he contemplates the validity of his faith while searching for people he met at *The Forum*. On the run to keep his family safe, he uncovers a devious scheme perpetuated by his company.

Adam's Bones

When the original Adam's bones are unearthed outside Cairo, Egypt, archeologist Dr. Erika Gustav becomes the target of a dangerous group of wealthy New Agers called The Ladder Club. As an employee of a Christian foundation collecting biblical artifacts, Erika eventually solves the mythical mystery surrounding information derived from *The Lost Books of the Bible*, her findings reinforcing her strong belief that Jesus Christ is Lord.

Out of Time: The Vanderbilt Incident

Vanderbilt University students in Nashville, Tennessee, meet weekly for Bible study and prayer. When Charlie discovers a mysterious bookmark in his Bible pointing to a historical Scripture when God altered time, he questions if today is *yesterday?* The group's investigation into the phenomena throws up red flags for the Feds. Members of the group are targeted as a threat to world security. Underlying the explosive sci-fi plot seethes the conflict between two major world religions, Christianity and Islam. What happens next is always unexpected.

Tomorrow's Promise

Trouble is a double-edged sword for Jolene Salisbury as she fights ovarian cancer while coping with a failing marriage. On a quest to revisit past family grievances, she leaves her husband and career job behind and returns to Charlotte, Tennessee, where she bonds with Nancy Blake, a young mother with five children. Together, they resolve problems and achieve happiness.

View Sue's website at www.resdawn.net

Dedicated to Seekers
Who choose to intimately know God

Contents

♥

"For he knows how we are formed, he remembers that we are dust," Psalm 103:14.

1

Dust to Dust

"**WATCH OUT FOR THE** dust under the bed," my mother warned me as a small child. "You can never tell who is coming or going." Of course, she was teasing as she ran the dust mop over the dusty hardwood floors while I trailed her around the house looking.

Young and impressionable, I was irresistibly attached to my mother's coattail at age five. Her words rang true to a child's ears. As I grew older, I occasionally wondered about *that* dust. More particularly, what is life all about? Why am I here? Why did she say that?

Clouds intrigued me as a preschooler. That glorious congregation of white, fluffy cottony stuff floating above me in a huge sea of flag blue sky! Wow! Hands tucked behind my head for support, I lay on my back in the tall green grass, beholding the expanse above me, wondering where I fit in. Mother told me that God lived out there somewhere in space. One day I would have the opportunity to visit Heaven, but living took a long time.

As I grew into my teens, time seemed to move faster. Days were shorter. There was never enough night to sleep longer or time to get things I wanted done.

Life comes in all forms, shapes, sizes, and colors. An indeterminate number of animals and plants coexist with people in a beautiful habitat called Earth. Each species competes for space, air, water, and nourishment.

Only the fittest and fierce of its kind survive.

At birth, each individual begins his or her journey through life. It's an exhilarating experience, constantly changing with aging and surrounding circumstances.

Of all God's creations, it is believed by most people that only humans possess an eternal soul. But like all other life forms, we have a limited lifespan before we return to dust, and the next generation of our species takes control over the planet. So the life cycle continues.

It's reported the human body is sixty-five percent water and the rest proteins and trace elements. When the body dies, it decays into dust. A quicker solution is cremation. So, it seems my mother was prophetic.

Scientists tell us that our human genetics reveal at what junctures in life we'll experience illness. I don't know about you, but I'd rather take life as it comes.

Observation of life suggests that some people are extremely fortunate while others receive their unfair share of ill-fated circumstances that lead to heartaches. Failures to achieve goals often threaten to drown the human spirit. Dreams can be dashed in a heartbeat.

People sometimes get discouraged when faced with difficulties. In self-destructive ways, they choose to live in disastrous ways. In an act of punishing themselves they focus on past mistakes and poor choices rather than construct a future that will benefit them in positive ways.

Some people view life as empty and not worth living, often discounting the impact of their actions on family and friends. Life is not meant to be lived solo. It is not always easy. But humans are wired to congregate and seek deeper meanings in life rather than just existing.

Dust: is it coming or going?

A great deal happens in between the coming and the going. The Bible has much to say about life.

Christ's disciple Peter said it this way: *"All men are like grass, and all their glory is like the flowers of the field; the grass withers and the flowers fall, but the word of the Lord stands forever"* (1 Peter 1: 24-25).

King Solomon, wise ruler over Israel, said this: *"The race is not to the swift or the battle to the strong, nor does food come to the wise or wealth to the brilliant or favor to the learned; but time and chance happen to them all"* (Ecclesiastes 9:11).

♥

"O Lord my God, you are very great; you are clothed with splendor and majesty," Psalm 104:1, the Bible.

2

Our Creator and the Bible

NO MATTER HOW YOU picture our Creator, He is more than you might imagine! God created the **SEEN** from things **UNSEEN.** That includes every universe, galaxy, star, planet, and life form that exists. With intelligence that far exceeds ours, our Creator has no beginning or end. Positioned outside earth's timeline in a place called Heaven, He sees and knows **ALL.**

Astronomy enthusiasts propose that the universe is so expansive other worlds must exist. Some suggest that alien life forms have visited earth in times past. They came to investigate us for reasons yet to be determined.

Confusion over who has it right exists today. Is the Bible's Creation Story true, or has science proven otherwise? The biblical account is miraculous. God made it **ALL** in six days and rested on the seventh.

Scientists who study rock fossils favor the gradual development of life over millions of years. This theory is called Evolution. However God fashioned our world, He utilized the earth's unique chemical components, or elements. John 1: 3 states, *"Through him all things were made; with him nothing was made that has been made."*

The Word of God in its present accepted form came together during the third century as scribes discerned what writings were factual from those whimsical thoughts of interested parties. There was so much information floating around that not all content could be included. Some biblical accounts in print today have been repudiated by skeptics. Some believe that Jesus didn't die, that His followers sneaked Him out of the country. Others contest his immaculate birth, doubting any mother could be a virgin. Confusion over which scenario is correct fosters doubt among people.

From the beginning of time, God inspired certain individuals to record incidents that demonstrate His personal contact and relationship with mankind. The Bible is collection of writings, a prophetic-history book that encompasses the past, present, and future.

Biblical scholars divide this information into the Old and New Testaments. Those who take time to read God's Word and meditate on it are changed as one's perspective is drastically altered. The desire to serve the omniscient, all-powerful Creator exponentially increases as the Bible becomes the unveiling tool for knowledge.

God hasn't changed and never will. He isn't moved by mankind's actions, good or bad. He's always been more interested in spiritual maturity than physical comfort. In the long haul, our Creator is mentoring us, seeking relationships, and grooming us for Heaven.

Not everyone today embraces Christianity or believes Jesus Christ is the only Son of God. But every religious idea spawned by man's imagination has included a connection between the physical mind and a supreme intelligence. Most people recognize that a higher force exists, some entity deserving their attention, if not worship. The ongoing conflict over religious truth has spawned wars and perpetrated as much evil as good.

~

Four hundred years separate the Old Testament from the New. These so-called "silent years" are defined by events, literature, and social forces that shaped the world into which Jesus Christ would be born.

Unnaturally conceived by the overshadowing of the Holy Spirit, God's seed was placed in the womb of the Virgin Mary. Jesus was sent into the world for a specific purpose, to reunite mankind with their Creator.

Except for a comment about Jesus going to the Temple at age twelve, little is revealed in the Bible about his childhood. Yet, endowed with a godly wisdom, Jesus begins his ministry at age thirty-three, jump-starting it by selecting twelve unlikely disciples, most unlearned.

These trainees will travel about the countryside beside Jesus, witnessing His miracles and discovering how God wants people to live. The Twelve will eventually be forerunners of Christ's eternal church.

While demonstrating spiritual gifts, Jesus taught a new wave of thought, to love your neighbor as yourself as well as worship the only true God. Along the way, He heals illnesses, diseases, raises the dead, and delivers people from evil influences. Casting demons out of fortunetellers didn't win Jesus any favor with handlers.

Many people loved Jesus and trusted His message. His life ended when crucified on a Roman cross for sins He did not commit. Labeled in the New Testament as the Second Adam, Jesus sacrificed His life in order to restore mankind to their former Garden-of-Eden status. His sacrificial blood offering in a heavenly temple was the act of grace that allows people to enter Heaven.

No person of any age is excluded.

After Jesus' body rested three days inside a sealed tomb outside Jerusalem, God the Father bodily resurrected Him. Not fully glorified, Jesus appeared and spent time with many of His followers. To prove He was both human and God's Son, Jesus ate meals on occasions. Before ascending in a cloud into Heaven, He removed the Old Testament saints from Satan's stronghold and carried them with Him. Satan was cast down, beaten by Jesus' act of grace, forever condemned.

Now, with the New Gospel installed, the Holy Spirit would become a guide to Jesus' followers. Empowered by God's Spirit, the Third personality of the Trinity, Jesus' ragtag group of twelve disciples began preaching and writing about their evangelistic experiences.

Matthew, Mark, Luke, and John recorded many facts about Jesus' life, His teachings and miracles. They established churches throughout the known world.

Others who knew Jesus, or had heard about Him, penned letters to first-century churches or testified of their faith experiences. Late in the century, a Jew named Saul became a strong advocate for Christian persecution.

Saul was not always a follower of Jesus. He belonged to an elite group of Jews who respected and loved God. Saul believed this new wave of religious thought was blasphemy. But Jesus had other plans for him.

After a dramatic encounter with the risen Christ while traveling on the Road to Damascus to Jerusalem, Saul was blinded and ready to hear the truth. He was healed after a priest prayed over him. Embracing his new mission, he carried this Good News to the Gentiles.

~

More than two-thousand years have passed since Jesus was crucified, resurrected, and ascended into Heaven. Created in God's image, wrapped in ever-changing flesh defined by genetic programming, hope springs as individuals realize that God freely offers His indwelling Holy Spirit to those who confess Jesus Christ as Lord. His purposes for humankind are timeless.

Generation after generation, our Heavenly Father oversees our daily struggles, our crazy day-to-day survival routines to gain access to water, food, and shelter. But taking care of our physical needs is never enough to satisfy our eternal soul. Humans are spiritually wired and constantly seek to know the reason we exist.

God recognizes our motives. He cannot be fooled, manipulated, controlled, or cast away by anyone or anything. Ultimately, He'll judge our acts of existence.

Empowered by the Holy Spirit, and freed from the practice of religious rituals, Christians born again through God's grace receive all the benefits Heaven offers, including spiritual gifts granted to the apostles, prophets, evangelists, pastors, and teachers of Jesus' day.

As time progressed, many faithful followers would record their experiences with Jesus, so many testimonies that it was impossible to contain them in one book.

Some theologians believe only a select few of those spiritual gifts granted to first-century Christians is valid today. They accept only a partial impartation of God's anointed gifts. Discerning the truth is often difficult.

Is Jesus God's *only* Son? Is the Bible true?

Can a person experience God's Presence?

Hopefully, this book will answer your questions.

♥

"As for man, his days are like grass, he flourishes like a flower of the field; the wind blows over it and it is gone, and its place remembers it no more," Psalm 103:15-16, the Bible.

3

Our Human Estate

AFTER DECADES OF LIVING I have glimpsed beyond my own personal existence to consider how God views mankind. To me, a few basic principles appear standard. The time and place of our birth, our parents, and our ethnic heritage are not our choices. We're born into the world with a physical body that has limitations, and an intelligent mind that's like a clean slate waiting for instructions. And we're granted a window of time for making choices that will not only affect how we live, but those around us. Life is an adventure to explore.

Basically, most people prefer to live good, decent lives. They desire to be appreciated by other people. But there's a fly in the batter, as my mother often said when things didn't go right. It's called "evil" and it's ever-present in our world. This evil wars against every good thought, good deed, and holy desire.

Evil was present in the world when you arrived and cannot be ignored. *"Be self-controlled and alert. Your enemy the devil prowls around like a roaring lion looking for someone to devour"* (1 Peter 5:8). I despise opposition, don't you?

But it's not just our fight. Satan's war with God started long before God created our world. Your enemy and mine was once an archangel in Heaven.

Satan has been described as beautiful, magnificent, and gifted. He led worship in Heaven but pride stole his serenity as he tested God's authority by amassing a third of the angelic host to make a run on God's throne.

After failing to achieve equity with God, Satan was cast down to the earth before Adam and Eve arrived in the Garden. As much as you and I prefer to ignore this evil One, we can't. He won't let us alone while we live on earth. *Ever!* He despises mankind, God's unique creation, and is even angrier now that he's suffered final defeat at the cross of Jesus, who rose from the dead and sits at the right hand of His Father and ours.

The struggle between God and Satan for human souls is ongoing. Revelation 12: 7-10 and 12 says this: *"And there was a war in heaven. Michael and his angels fought against the dragon, and the dragon and his angels fought back. But he (devil) was not strong enough, and they lost their place in heaven. The great dragon was hurled down—that ancient serpent called the devil, or Satan, who leads the whole world astray. He was hurled to the earth, and his angels with him . . . But woe to the earth and the sea, because the devil has gone down to you! He is filled with fury, because he knows that his time is short."*

♥

"The Mighty One, God, the Lord, speaks and summons the earth from the rising of the sun to the place where it sets. From Zion, perfect in beauty, God shines forth. Our God comes and will not be silent," Psalm 50:1-3.

4

God's Awesome Presence

DURING OLD TESTAMENT DAYS God spoke directly to a chosen few. These anointed individuals called prophets relayed God's message to Israel's kings or priests. God's message often interrupted the course of Israel's destiny. Always instructive, often encouraging, sometimes judgmental or prophetic, truth was spoken.

Surprising to some, Jesus appeared occasionally in those olden times as the pre-incarnate Christ, foreshadowing His future role in His Father's eternal kingdom. One such occasion was a manifestation as he posed as Melchizedek, recorded in *Genesis 14: 18-20.*

Abraham, then called Abram, recognized this man from Salem (modern day Jerusalem) as both king and priest, then bowed down and offered him a tenth of everything he owned. Later, Jesus appeared as one of the three angels who visited Abram's desert campsite to deliver the message that his wife Sarah would have a son in a year's time. At age eighty-nine, Sarah laughed at the idea of motherhood, a faithless thought detected by the pre-incarnate Jesus, who quickly reprimanded her.

Generations pass and God selects a young man named Moses to deliver His chosen tribe of Israel from Egyptian bondage. Found floating in a basket, the infant Moses is rescued by the Pharaoh's daughter but cared for by his own birth mother. As a young adult, he becomes alarmed when assigned to free the Israelite nation from bondage. After witnessing an Egyptian soldier mistreating an Israelite slave, Moses murders the soldier and flees into the desert for the next forty years.

But God's call remains firm. When Moses witnesses God speaking from a burning bush, he is ready to obey.

Moses returns to Egypt. With the support of his brother Aaron, who speaks better, Moses follows God's instructions to the letter. With each refusal of the Pharaoh to *Let My People Go*, he illustrates God's power by raising his staff and instigating a series of ten plagues.

While leading a million or more displaced Israelites through the Sinai Desert on their way to the land promised to Abraham, Moses declares in Deuteronomy 4:7: *"What other nation is so great as to have their gods near them the way the Lord our God is near us whenever we pray to him?"*

Unfortunately, Israel's leader never steps on that slice of chosen property because of disobedience. Moses stuck a rock to get water when God instructed him to speak to it. Afterwards, he ventures into the mountains alone and his body was never found.

We learn from a New Testament writer that Satan once disputed with God over Moses' body.

In another incident, Elijah and Moses appear to Jesus during His "transfiguration" on Mount Hermon. The disciples, Peter, James and John are also present. Wherever Moses dwells, he's well and alive and active.

God spoke to other sons in the Israelite tribe. One dominant figure is a talented young man named Daniel.

Along with other bright Israelites, he was captured in Jerusalem by the Babylonian army and exiled in what is now Iraq. Though a mere slave, Daniel's unique gift for interpreting dreams becomes recognized. After studying Jewish writings, he discovers that Father Abraham foretold their Jewish captivity four-hundred years earlier, and that the captivity would end after seventy years.

While fasting in sackcloth, covered in ashes, Daniel petitions God to deliver His chosen people from slavery. In Daniel 9: 17-18-19, he asks the Lord for favor. *"O Lord, listen! O Lord, forgive! O Lord, hear and act!"*

In verses 20-23, while Daniel was praying and confessing his sins before God, the angel Gabriel appears to him in a vision: *"Daniel, I have now come to give you insight and understanding. A soon as you began to pray, an answer was given, which I have come to tell you, for you are highly esteemed. Therefore, consider the message and understand the vision."* Daniel then receives a revelation of future world events that catapults us to the end of the Bible.

As Abraham predicted, the Israelite nation was freed from slavery after seventy years and allowed to return home. Since that time, Jews have struggled to occupy Israel while other religions also claim a heritage to the property. Wars have been fought over its ownership.

Could it be this Promised Land represents a deeper meaning for Christians today? Does this most coveted property signify a future dwelling place for Christians? A safe-haven where followers of Jesus will dwell eternally secure after wandering the barren landscape of life. Ultimately, is our promised land called *Heaven?*

♥

"For to us a child is born, to us a son is given, and the government will be on his shoulders. And he will be called Wonderful, Counselor, Mighty God, Everlasting Father, Prince of Peace," Isaiah 9:6, the Bible.

5

God's Good News

FAST FORWARD TO THE last half of the first century. Jesus Christ, who proclaimed to be God's only Son and lived on earth as a man for thirty-three years, has been crucified under Roman rule for crimes He did not commit. He was bodily resurrected after three days in a tomb and has ascended into Heaven to sit at the right hand of His Father. His work on earth is complete!

Jesus' ministry on earth is now left in the hands of common folk, called His Church. The New Testament is about to be written by those Jesus has impacted with His divine Presence. His Twelve Disciples have learned the principles required for salvation through grace and are willing to share this Good News with others.

Empowered by the Holy Spirit to perform miracles as they move about preaching and teaching, the disciples of Jesus Christ will establish new churches wherever they go so people can learn about God and obtain the gift of salvation. Born-again Christians, indwelled by God's Holy Spirit, are granted spiritual gifts that will enable them to demonstrate God's awesome power.

Opposition from many advocates of the Old Laws remains. Much bloodshed will occur before the Christ's Church establishes a firm foundation on earth. Many Jews refuse to accept the concepts taught by Jesus.

The Apostle Paul writes these words to a new church plant: *"Devote yourselves to prayer, being watchful and thankful. And pray for us, too, that God may open a door for our message, so that we may proclaim the mystery of Christ, for which I am in chains," (Colossians 4:2-3)*

Prayer is central to the Christian faith. It is the way a person praises and thanks God, offers petitions, and seeks advice. Jesus taught the Twelve to pray in this way: *"Our Father Who art in heaven, hallowed be Thy name. Thy kingdom come, Thy will be done on earth as it is in heaven. Give us this day our daily bread, and forgive our trespasses as we forgive those who trespass against us. And deliver us from evil for Thine is the kingdom, the power, and the glory forever."*

The best of the Good News is that you can be a recipient of God's grace, and fully cooperate in His kingdom on earth. Grace will open the door to spiritual gifts. You will have the opportunity to demonstrate God's power on earth and bring many souls to Christ.

♥

"Can you fathom the mysteries of God? Can you probe the limits of the Almighty?" Job 11:7, the Bible.

6

God's Mysterious Ways

Ruth tells this story . . .

THE STILLNESS IN THE cemetery was broken with wracking sobs coming out of my mouth from deep inside. "Lord, I have to know!" I pleaded that day as I sat on the ground by my mother's grave. "Lord, did she accept you before she died? Is she in heaven with you?"

Earlier that spring, Mom was not feeling well so she set up an appointment with a local physician. After examining her, the doctor diagnosed that she suffered from influenza. Weeks passed and Mom's condition did not improve so she went to see the doctor who had performed her cancer surgery five years before.

While performing exploratory surgery, he found a massive cancerous growth that had invaded Mom's entire abdominal area. Given only six weeks to live was a devastating report for my mother and our family.

At the time I was taking a summer class at a Bible college in another state when I received the awful news. I dropped everything and rushed home to be at Mom's side. When she came home from the hospital, my siblings and I convinced her to undergo chemotherapy.

I viewed the pain on my mother's face as medical personnel went from arm to arm to ankle to find a vein that would support an IV firm enough to serve as a port for the chemotherapy. Mom was tough and never let on she was afraid. As a relatively new Christian, I firmly believed Jesus could heal my Mom. But I didn't recall her ever attending the Lutheran church where my sister and I went. Aware her time was limited I prayed and asked the Lord the best way for me to witness to her.

Mom needed to know Jesus and accept Him as her personal savior, so she'd make it into Heaven. And I needed to know we would be together eternally.

The next few weeks following surgery, Mom had many visitors and outings with friends and family. It seemed we had a continual full house. One day, as I drove Mom around town to purchase bedding plants for her flower gardens, we had a chance to talk.

It was a good day. We laughed together at the silliest things. At age of 22, I thrived at this experience, a relationship I had always dreamed of having with my mother. When I parked the car in the garage after our last shopping spree, Mom looked seriously at me.

"Will you teach me to drive?" she asked.

I was shocked and amazed that she'd asked for my help, but mostly I was proud of her. At age sixty-four, diagnosed with terminal cancer, Mom not only wanted to dress up her flowerbeds, but wanted to learn to drive.

So I agreed to teach her as soon as I returned from college after checking on things. The following day, while I was packing to head back to college, the Lord gave me a nudge: *Go talk to her.* She wasn't feeling well and lying in bed, so I sat at her side and began telling her about the saving grace of Jesus Christ.

My words tumbled out fast as I recalled how I came to accept Jesus as my Lord and Savior. That decision had turned my life around, so I shared with Mom God's desire that none should perish but *all* experience the gift of grace and eternal life. If she would only believe and pray to Jesus for forgiveness, He'd come into her life.

I asked Mom that day if she'd pray the prayer of salvation with me before I left for college. She declined, but I still left with a peace from the Lord that she had the truth and would eventually accept Him when ready.

While at college, I talked with family members daily about Mom's condition. Pulled in two directions, I felt God had a reason for me attending Bible College. Still, I longed to go home and be with my mother.

I prayed about what I should do. This was my last opportunity to care for Mom the rest of her life.

It was five weeks after Mom's prognosis of cancer when my prayer partner and I sat down to seek God on behalf of Mom's illness and what Jesus would have me do. I asked Him to speak to Mom's heart and remind her of the salvation prayer I'd shared with her the day before I left for college. "Dear Lord, don't let Mom die without first accepting Your great gift of salvation!"

A tremendous peace invaded my spirit that evening and later as I lay down to sleep for the night. At 1:30 a.m., I received the call that Mom had passed away.

So I went home.

It was a huge funeral, beautiful with colorful flowers everywhere. Like a family reunion with all seven siblings gathered under one roof. We could not believe how many friends and relatives came to say goodbye to Mom.

I would love saying I held it all together, that I stood firm in the peace God had granted me. But I didn't.

I lost it at the graveside, alone and sobbing, recalling how Jesus told the thief on the cross beside Him that he would be with him in paradise that very day.

I truly believe when you die you either go to be with Jesus instantly, or will be forever separated from Him.

A few weeks later, I returned to Mom's gravesite, still wondering, still seeking an answer from God.

Is my mother saved?

At this silent place of the resting dead, where once I picked wild strawberries as a child, I contemplated an answer. Here was not where I wanted to be. But here, I needed to be. Where is my mother? I needed to know.

I desperately needed to grieve Mom's death and seek God's Presence for solace. My sobs came swift, out of my deepest sorrow as I asked the Lord again, "Please tell me. Let me know. I need to know."

Is Mom with you, Jesus?

In the cool stillness of that afternoon, a warm breeze blew across my face, startling me at first. I opened my eyes and glanced around at the green blades of grass. They weren't stirring. I scanned the tree tops. No breeze there. Maybe, I only imagined the wind.

So I closed my eyes again and asked, "Lord . . .?" the gentle warm breeze blew across my face again.

At that moment I knew that God, King of the Universe, the Holy one of Israel, had heard my prayer and was answering with this gentle touch of a breeze.

God's Holy Spirit, the very *Ruach* breath of God, blew on my face that moment and infused me with an answer. *Yes!* Mom is with Jesus in Heaven!

I was later told that Mom had worn and held onto her cross necklace while in the hospital during her final days. It was then she must have accepted the Lord Jesus Christ as her Savior. With this kiss of gentle breeze,

God's confirming Holy Spirit Presence gave me reassurance that Mom was in Heaven. My tears of fear and pain immediately turned into rejoicing as I accepted the truth: we would one day be reunited in Heaven.

~

Ruth's story illustrates that God is always watching over us and knows what we need at the time we need it. Even the wind is compelled to obey Him, illustrated in the Bible when Jesus silenced the wind in a dangerous storm while riding in a boat with His disciples.

God desires a personal relationship with each of us. In the midst of life's sometimes difficult journey, splattered with occasional surprises and exuberant joys, we sometimes receive a promised peace that challenges our perspective. It's our divine journey of faith.

♥

"For the wages of sin is death, but the gift of God is eternal life in Christ Jesus our Lord," Romans 6:23, the Bible.

7

God's Redemptive Nature

IN NOVEMBER OF 1983 while living in Stone Mountain, Georgia, I became licensed to sell real estate properties. Just starting to engage in my new trade, I was diagnosed with Graves Disease, a condition whereby the thyroid gland overproduces the enzyme thyroxin. I experienced nervousness, weight loss, muscle weakness, and fatigue. Like a car out of gas, I was running on fumes. If not treated, the disease would incapacitate or kill me.

In March the following year, two things happened. I ingested a radioactive tablet that destroyed my thyroid gland and learned that my husband's job had transferred him to Jackson, Mississippi. Both events profoundly impacted our lives. My three children were as upset over moving as I was. After two-and-a-half years, we were established in our community, both at church and schools, had developed friendships, and loved where we lived. While my husband was elated with the promotion, my children and I were emotionally blown away.

My daughter Karen, about to embark on her senior year in high school, was on a cheerleader squad projected to win state awards. Secretly, she plotted with a friend to stay behind. "No," her father said, "You go where the money goes." So that was settled.

My eldest daughter, a freshman in a Georgia college, didn't want us to move since she'd no longer qualify for reduced instate tuition. And our son Lee, about to enter the ninth grade, was unhappy to leave his friends.

In the midst of my body reacting to a drug that destroyed my thyroid gland, my husband insisted on driving to Jackson to preview properties. Complicating matters, I contracted a stomach bug accompanied with symptoms of influenza just before we left the house.

On the ride over to Jackson, I collapsed in the back seat of our car thinking I should just go ahead and die. We arrived hours later and spent the night in a motel.

Spring was blossoming in Mississippi that first day we looked at houses. Our real estate agent showed us three my husband had previously selected. Feeling awful and wanting to get the house-hunting process behind us, I recall sitting in the floor of the vacant den of the first house we looked at and telling my husband I'd take it.

We did view other properties, but my first choice turned out to be our best. We packed up and left Stone Mountain in April of 1984 and moved into our new home on the Reservoir, leaving behind Sharon, who was completing her first year of college. My senior and ninth grader registered for school and we resumed our lives.

From the back deck, we had a wonderful view of the Reservoir, a man-made lake that covers acres. As soon as our house was in order, I was ready to resume work.

Except The Mississippi Real Estate Commission refused to transfer my license since the state did not reciprocate with Georgia's requirements. I would need to take all my classes again, a huge job setback for me.

I should have been elated with my husband's promotion and our purchase of a brand-new home, except for unresolved personal issues that plagued me.

As months went by, I began to scrutinize my relationship with Jesus and to assess why I didn't feel His Presence as I once had. The task of introspective surgery was brutal but deemed necessary. I realized that sin had a taken root in me and I needed to dig it out.

Back then, this is what happened . . .

My spiritual problem began in 1979 while living in Memphis, Tennessee. During that era of my life, I was not teaching school since my children participated in so many sports and church activities outside of school.

Most days I did chores around the house, shopped, or visited with friends. One morning, a neighbor invited me to take a ride with her to visit a friend.

I didn't realize the friend living in south Memphis was a spiritual reader. After the psychic laid out the Tara cards and read them for Carol, she grasped my right palm, studied the lines, and began telling me about myself, prophesying that I had a bright future.

I was destined to become a well-known novelist. At the time I was only penning songs, so the news was stunning. *No*, she insisted, *you will write novels.*

Carol and I returned to our homes and life resumed its normal routine. Soon after visiting the psychic, I had a dream about a woman falling through a glass floor and seeing a ghost in her basement. It was the premise of my first secular novel. Exhausted after six weeks of furiously describing the images flashing across my mind, I finished that novel and began writing a second one.

By then, the Christmas season was approaching and I was mentally exhausted. Spring of 1980 arrived I wanted to visit Carol's psychic friend again. Since she'd helped me recognize my gift in penning novels, I didn't see anything wrong with talking to her.

How could one more visit hurt?

The psychic was proud to learn that I had written two novels. It was time to take my gift to the next level. I didn't know what that meant. She removed a little black book of prayers from her desk drawer and said I needed to pray to an unknown god for guidance.

Well, that idea didn't sit too well with my biblical background. There is no other God but Jehovah, I recalled. "No, I can't do that," I declined.

"But you must, if you are to achieve greater fame."

Suddenly, the dark room in which I sat wrapped around my spirit like a tight rope. The large picture of Jesus hanging on the wall behind the psychic's desk didn't gel with the round crystal ball. I knew that I'd made a terrible mistake in coming.

"I appreciate your help, really, but . . ." all I wanted to do was get out of there. The atmosphere was suffocating. I felt ashamed, like I'd betrayed Jesus.

So Carol and I left the psychic's house. She didn't understand my reaction to the little book. But I knew from reading the Bible that contacting false prophets was forbidden. By September I was battling depression.

I once crouched in my dark closet during the day and prayed to die. The prophetic words of the psychic circled my mind and created fear. Would I have to live out what I had sown? Would her prophecies come true?

Halloween approached and I was scheduled to perform one of my original children's songs at my Baptist church. When the day for the Fall Fest event arrived, I was too sick to function. Nevertheless, I went down to the church then turned around and came home.

November thirteen, the day I turned forty years old, I lay in bed that night restlessly tossing from fever and head congestion. My doctor diagnosed my malady as influenza and prescribed no antibiotics. Unable to breathe, I felt my spirit lifting out of my body.

"Am I dying, Lord?" I asked God in prayer.

Where was my family? They were all downstairs watching television. If Jesus had a plan for my life, it was time for Him to say so. Death lurked at my bedside.

Certainly, I had defiled the Holy Spirit by my blatant actions in contacting a psychic. I prayed for forgiveness and felt a release. Then fell back asleep.

From that point on I was better. By January 1981 I felt more human, but the illness left me with an irregular heartbeat. Come spring, my husband's job transferred us to Stone Mountain, Georgia. Then we'd moved to Mississippi. So here I was, looking back on mistakes.

My present dilemma . . .

Not all of the psychic's prophecies over my life were positive. During my time living in Georgia I struggled with fear and unfaithfulness to my spouse. I once dreamed an unknown spirit entered our house as the back door blew open from a strong wind. I came under the temptation of sin. How could I receive forgiveness?

I speculated on my new walk with Jesus in 1984. What could I offer Him now? Bygone years had nearly destroyed my confidence in holiness. I felt empty and ready for the filling of the Holy Spirit. It was time to set my life straight. God wasn't going to change so I must.

I woke up early each morning to read my Bible and pray before going to work. But the weight of guilt persisted as I digressed over past mistakes. I desperately needed to know I had been freed from the psychic's prophetic curses. No longer writing secular novels, I placed all four boxed manuscripts in storage. I wanted to be finished with the feeling of regret and move forward with representing Christ in positive ways.

Deliverance was unexpected . . .

I ventured outdoors one spring morning of 1986, climbed into my car with an armful of real estate materials, and switched on the motor. Instantly, out of the radio came the crisp base voice of a Chicago pastor.

"If you have been defiled by a false prophet, go back in your house and kneel by your bed, God is about to forgive you." Though it seemed impossible, I felt that the evangelist was speaking directly to me. So, I obeyed and went back into my house and knelt by my bed.

Weeping and baring my soul before God on my knees, I asked Jesus to forgive me for so many transgressions. Moments later, I felt a release, like a heavy weight lifting off my body as the incredible love of Jesus cleansed me. It was the beginning of a new walk where God became an intimate friend to me.

Jesus began speaking to me through the words of the Bible, revelation, dreams, and songs. By the following July, I was called to Christian city-jail ministry in the most unusual way, which I will later address.

♥

"The Lord detests the sacrifice of the wicked, but the prayer of the upright pleases him," Proverbs 15: 8, the Bible.

8

God Hears Prayers

I WAS LIVING IN JACKSON, Mississippi, and working as a real estate agent. It was Friday, completing a week of new houses held open by agents in celebration of Builder's Week. April showers were in progress that afternoon. Skies were dark and somber with the weight of clouds as dusk collapsed over the city.

I was headed home, grateful to be finished with my busy workday, and looking forward to enjoying a quiet meal with my husband at a seafood restaurant.

Halfway home, my car-phone rang. It was our company secretary calling. "What can I do for you, Amy?" I asked as noisy raindrops clawed at my windshield, countered by hard swishing wipers. I could barely see the highway unspooling in front of me.

"Judy can't open her listing at that new Reservoir subdivision," she informed me. "Since you live close, do you mind opening the house and staying for an hour?"

I heard the intensity in Amy's voice. At this late hour, on a Friday, most people had plans set.

But Judy needed my help. Still . . . "Amy, it's pouring down rain!" At first I protested. "No one in their right mind is looking at houses at this late hour."

It was my best attempt to avoid the task.

33

But Amy insisted that the listing must be opened or the builder would be upset. "Okay . . ." I reluctantly agreed to do it. "But only for an hour," I qualified.

I drove home first, dumped my real estate supplies in the house, and left my husband a note saying I'd be back around seven. Then I headed off to Judy's listing.

The weather was terrible. Sitting in an empty house was not something I wanted to do.

"Why me . . .?" I asked God.

It became obvious that most reasonable agents had cancelled their open houses as I maneuvered through the muddy, empty subdivision streets. Not a soul was stirring, not even a mouse. No surprise there.

After retrieving the house key from the real-estate lockbox, I began walking through the two-story house, flipping on lights since it was nearly dark outdoors.

Seriously . . . I called out, "I'm here, Lord! Nobody's coming to see this house, Lord! I'm wasting time!"

Just as I completed turning on all the lights on the second floor, the front doorbell sounded.

"Humph, that's odd."

I hurried downstairs and opened the front door. A lady who appeared to be in her mid-thirties stood there half-drenched from the rain, her umbrella about to collapse on her from its weight. *What do I say?*

"Why are you here?"

Give me a break! I have more training than *that*.

"I don't know." She backed into the compact foyer, shaking out her limp umbrella on the porch landing before parking it in a corner and facing me.

Dumbfounded, I stood there, offering no reply.

"Well," she said, "I was sitting at my table in my house reading my Bible when God told me to get up and take a drive." A quizzical expression cloned her face.

That was my first clue God was up to something. At the time I was engaged in a city jail ministry so I'd heard God's whisperings before. But this encounter had my full attention. "Did you see our ad in the paper?"

"No," she replied.

We just looked at one another, both clueless.

"Were you just driving by and saw the lights on?"

"Yes, I did see the lights—that's why I stopped."

Okay, I thought to myself, *we're getting somewhere.*

"Is your current house for sell?" I inquired. "Is that why you're looking at new homes?" I probed deeper.

"No, that's not it." She told me her name. "I'm an attorney and my house is practically brand new."

At that point, I believe we both realized this was no ordinary situation. I shouldn't have even been there. It wasn't my listing. It was almost night and raining. And the streets in the subdivision were virtually empty. She shouldn't be here, either. Yet, we were.

"Well, since you're here you might as well see the house," I offered. "You might know of someone else who would be interested in buying it."

I gave her the once-over tour. Ten minutes later we were done. As we stood at the front door about to say our goodbyes, I asked, "Are you a Christian?"

"I am," she replied then told me how she'd accepted Jesus as her Savior while watching a preacher on TV delivering a sermon on tithing. "Bring all the tithes into the storehouse, and I will bless you, the Lord says."

Have you ever been struck with enlightenment? Suddenly, I knew why we were standing there. This woman, no prospective buyer, had no way of knowing that only five days before, on Monday morning during my prayer time, I had asked God if I could use $3,000 of my sales commissions to record a demo of my original gospel tunes instead of giving a tithe. This faithful Christian, selected by God, was delivering the answer to my question. "Bring all the tithes into the storehouse."

Justified at knowing my time given to Judy's house was worthwhile, I shared a bit of my own testimony in response to also reward her for time not wasted.

We shared in one of those God-defined moments together before parting, never to see one another again. Her obedience changed my monetary intent. The following Sunday, I gave my full tithe to our church.

But my blessing for obedience to God's Word did not immediately come to fruition. Nearly a year later, via a real estate associate, I heard about Frank Williams, a writer-singer who worked for a local recording company.

Since my associate was a friend of the producer, she gave me Frank's number and said to call him.

We spoke by phone and Frank agreed to hear some of my gospel tunes. Except, he was so busy we never seemed to set a time to meet. One day I decided to go over to the studio and take a chance I would catch him in. The secretary told me Frank was out, and she didn't know when he'd be back. Foiled again, I thought.

I was walking out of the studio when we suddenly faced one another. I said hello to Frank. He said "hi" then I sang a little bit of a new tune I'd written the day before. Frank liked the "hook" or theme so much he told me to put the song on tape and bring it over.

In the weeks to come, Frank changed some of the melody and lyrics to fit his group's gospel style. "Heaven is All Sold Out" was recorded by the *Jackson Southernaires* and released on an album for airplay.

I still have an album copy. No doubt God hears prayers. Our Creator rewards obedience but not always in the manner we anticipate. Sometimes it takes longer than five days to get a response. *Ask and ye shall receive.*

When God deems the time is right, His answer is on our doorstep. But if we don't listen, how will we hear?

♥

"Is anything too hard for the Lord?" Genesis 18:14, the Bible.

9

God Revolves Difficult Situations

LATE SPRING OF 1987 I received a call from prospective sellers and was invited over to discuss my real estate marketing plan. The prospect of a new listing is always exciting. As I sat down with Cecil and Deb in their living room, and learned of their unique situation, I realized why their home hadn't sold. They lived yards away from a noisy highway most buyers avoided.

Although the couple had offers from customers desiring to rezone their property for business purposes, they couldn't sell since subdivision guidelines restricted commercial transactions. Frustrated over their failure to sell their home, they needed professional guidance.

After going through several listing agencies during the past decade, a friend of theirs recommended they contact me for assistance. Curious as to why I was selected, I discovered a friend of Deb's recommended me since I was a Christian and prayed over my listings.

I assured Cecil and Deb I would pray for their house to sell, but could do no more than other agents had done, which is to advertise and place the property in the Multiple Listing Book. The Internet was not yet active.

But they seemed hopeful anyhow.

There were health issues, too. Cecil had contracted multiple sclerosis years before and found it difficult to negotiate the steep stairs leading up to the second-story bedrooms. They needed a one-level residence.

Deb was desperate to get Cecil in a more livable situation. However, they required a certain equity amount out of the sale in order to buy another property. Thus, their list price was non-negotiable.

Realizing the burden the couple bore, I trusted this was a property God wanted me to list. In conclusion, we prayed together. I told them I'd be back to measure the house and record all the information I'd need.

As time passed, potential purchasers viewed the property and would have purchased it for a business. Both the sellers and I were frustrated as Cecil's condition worsened. I contacted the committee in charge of monitoring the subdivision restrictions but made no headway. I told my sellers I didn't know what else to do.

Then God intervened months later when a truck struck the house and rocked the foundation. The sellers collected $20,000, performed the necessary repairs, and reduced the price in line with what was left over.

Yet, no offers came forward. A year passed and it was time to renew the listing. I informed Cecil and Deb that my husband was being transferred out of state and we were moving. I was sorry I had failed them.

The day the listing expired a sales associate, representing a new condominium development in Jackson, phoned the sellers and invited them out to see their model. The setup was perfect: a one-story condo with a postcard-sized yard. The owner even offered to trade homes, with the intention of renting theirs.

Conflicted over selling their home without me as their agent, Deb phoned to tell me what had happened.

I rejoiced with her and said to work out the contract, make the move. Our prayers had been answered.

By that time Cecil was having difficulty walking.

A week later, I received a call from the subdivision owner telling me that his agent was unable to work out a deal with the buyers since the transition was so emotionally challenging for them. Would I intervene and help put the contract together? I agreed, knowing it was probably the only opportunity the distressed couple would have to sell their home and make the move.

What a surprise when the owner offered to pay me the same commission he paid his listing agent!

After the contract on the condo was negotiated, the sale moved forward without a glitch. The day the contract was scheduled to close Cecil fell down the stairs at his house and was hospitalized. I took the closing papers to him for signing and finalized the sale.

As soon as feasible, the couple moved into the condo. I rejoice over how God works in answering prayer. First, I listed the house and prayed for them.

Later, a truck struck the house and they collected the insurance money, which allowed them to reduce the sales price. Then, with perfect timing, I ended the listing since our family was moving. Simultaneously, the sales agent contacted Cecil and Deb about seeing the condo.

It took all of these events to consummate the sale, none of which I could have orchestrated as a real estate agent. For Cecil and Deb, it was their miracle after years of praying. Meanwhile, God was mentoring me for a new adventure at the place where I never wanted to live.

~

Sharon had graduated from college, and was a maturing Christian. I recall one December in particular, when I accompanied her to Union, Mississippi, to attend a wedding. We arrived late afternoon on a cold, snowy

Friday, checked into the two-story motel, then ventured over to the church for a rehearsal dinner.

Ann, Sharon's friend from college days, was the bride. By 10:30 p.m. we were back at the motel, freezing from the icy snow and brisk wind.

"Hurry up, open the door!" I exclaimed from the second-story concrete landing as snow peppered down.

"The key won't turn in the lock," Sharon reported.

I wasn't pleased with the news. "Maybe you should go down to the office and request another key."

I waited outside our room, shivering and anxious to go to bed, while Sharon jaunted down the steps.

"What?" She came back looking miserable.

"The lady at the front desk said it's happened before—the lock's jammed. The last person who had this room couldn't get in until the next morning when the locksmith came with his tools," she explained.

"But that's unacceptable."

"Worse, my wedding attire is in there."

Sharon had an early morning breakfast with the bridal party. "That's troubling." I considered our options. "Did the gal at the desk have suggestions?"

"Yeah, she gave me a key to another room." Sharon glared at me. "What am I going to do, Mom?"

"Okay . . ." my eyes were wide open in speculation. "We'll just have to think of something."

Sharon brightened. "I know. I'll do what you did when you opened the door that time your elderly couple got stuck in that vacant HUD home in Slidell."

I smiled at my Christian daughter. That incident was a wild moment in history. I recall the steamy day in July when I scouted for an investment property in Slidell, Louisiana, with an elderly couple in their mid-seventies.

They were interested in foreclosures and I had one in mind. After accessing the real estate lockbox I retrieved the house key and opened the HUD house.

Having been vacant for awhile, the electricity was shut off and windows nailed down from the outside so it was hot and stuffy indoors and difficult to breathe.

I thought nothing of locking the door behind us to avoid any uninvited visitors. I just wanted us to be safe, no surprises. We hurriedly walked through the three-bedroom house and returned to the foyer.

I tried to turn the lock and it wouldn't budge.

"Can't get the door open?" My customer tried his luck with the door. "It's stuck. Any tools around?"

By that time, his wife appeared nervous.

"No, I said." It was a vacant house.

"Maybe someone will come around and check on us before long," his sweaty wife hopefully uttered.

"Maybe," I said, *in your dreams,* I thought.

It was a situation with the potential to turn deadly. We had no phones between the three of us. Our purses were locked in my car. My customers were elderly, him with a heart condition, and I was on the verge of panic.

Dear Lord, we really need Your help.

"What are we going to do?" the gentleman asked.

I thought about my options then answered, "I know you may think I'm crazy," I uttered, "but I'm going to lay my hand on the lock and ask Jesus to open it."

The couple looked at me strangely. Still, I placed my right hand on the stubborn door and started praying for it to open. "Now, you unlock it," I told my customer.

He reached over, with a skeptical expression playing on his face, and obediently twisted the rusted lock.

I reached for the knob. It turned and we stepped outdoors, relieved to be let out of our jailed situation.

"Well," his wife huffed as she inhaled a fresh breath of air, "if I ever need anyone to pray for me, I'll know who to call." That was what Sharon was talking about. So there we stood in the snowy weather, locked out of our motel room with all our clothes inside.

"You do it," I told my daughter. "You pray."

Sharon laid her right hand over the stubborn lock and commanded it to open in the name of Jesus then inserted the old-fashioned key in the lock.

Instantly, we stepped inside the room.

Using the motel phone, Sharon called the desk and reported that we would not need another room that night. Sharon went downstairs to return the alternate room key. When the desk attendant asked how we got in the room, she testified that prayer opened the door.

The lady remarked, "If I ever need someone to pray for me, I know who to call." And Sharon came to bed.

God, in the name of *Jesus,* isn't that obvious?

♥

*"Every good and perfect gift is from above, coming down from
the Father of the heavenly lights, who does not change like
shifting shadows," James 1:17, the Bible.*

10

God's Perfect Gifts

WITH SEARS PAYING FOR our move to Slidell, I was
scheduled to see properties with a Coldwell Banker agent
in late spring of 1988. Typical of south Louisiana
weather, it was already tropical-steamy hot.

It was raining hard the day I arrived. Although God
had warned me in my prayer time that we were moving,
I gasped at the ugly terrain in comparison to
Mississippi's lush rolling hills. Coming unglued, I turned
into the unhappy camper, dreading the move to a place I
already disliked. That first night in town, my tears
literally dripped in my food as my husband and I dined
at the motel restaurant. "This is a good position for
me," he happily proclaimed, thrilled with the promotion.

"Good for you," I was thinking since I would be
required to start all over again establishing myself as a
real estate sales agent. What a total bummer!

Later that first evening, when our real estate agent
called to confirm my appointment, I was so upset I
refused to speak with her. My husband said I was under
the weather. (Ha. Ha.) Then he confirmed with her that
I would be available the next morning to view houses.

Fortunately, the next morning turned bright and
sunny and warm. All smiles at a prospective sale,

Frances picked me up at the motel. "What do you want to see today?" she asked, bubbling with personality.

"I don't want to see any houses."

Moody . . . I was in a funk.

"Okay . . . what do you want to do?" She chuckled.

"I want to shop. Are there any good stores here?"

Slidell is a bedroom community of New Orleans. Situated on the North Shore of Lake Pontchartrain, the town and suburbs are populated by many industrious people working in the oil industry or in government jobs overseeing the New Orleans' International Port of Call.

Gause Boulevard, the main street, stretches from the Pearl River on the east to the only mall in town on the west. The surrounding terrain is flat and cluttered with commercial properties. Trees are sparse, not growing well in sandy soil. In one word, the town is *ugly*.

Frances didn't show me one house that first day in Slidell. Needless to say, she was attuned to my needs and soon became one of my best friends. I soon realized there was no new construction. Plummeting oil prices and the downturn of the economy had left few resale properties available for purchase.

Eventually, Frances put us in contact with a builder and we selected a suitable lot in a popular subdivision and began building. We moved into our new home on July 23, 1988. It was my youngest daughter's birthday.

A neighbor across the street brought a cake over to Karen since my kitchen was a clutter of packed boxes.

By late July, the sultry weather spawned three Gulf hurricanes that bullied their way through our area before we purchased flood insurance.

Soon after that, I passed the Louisiana real estate licensing test and joined a local Coldwell Banker.

Deciding I had no choice but to make the best of the move, I began working. My eldest daughter Sharon had graduated from college by then and stayed behind to work in Jackson. Karen was still in college, and our son Lee registered as a senior to attend a local high school.

The first day I was on phone duty at Coldwell Banker, it was a miserable rainy Saturday in late August. I sat down at the front desk to take phone-in ad calls and greet drop-in customers, thinking that no one in their right mind would be out in this weather looking for houses. Prepared for an uneventful morning, I was delighted when a curly-headed blond raced into the office, reached across the desk and grabbed my arm.

"I have to find a house today!" she cried out then collapsed her dripping umbrella. My day suddenly brightened as I faced my first customer on the job. Sue and her husband eventually purchased a house in my subdivision and we became best friends as time passed.

In September, Coldwell Banker was secretly sold to Latter and Blum, a local New Orleans' conglomerate. Many of the established agents left the company, upset over the manner in which the sale had transpired overnight. Since I was a new agent, I opted to stay with the new owners. Many of those disgruntled agents assigned their listings to me on a referral basis.

That first year in a new area I sold more than two million dollars in properties. God had given me several gifts that year. He had allowed Cecil and Deb's house in Jackson to sell, forewarned me of our move to south Louisiana, introduced me to my best friend, gave me a brand new house, and blessed my real estate business.

Gifts sometimes come in bundles, disbursed at unusual times. As Christians, we need to recognize God's interventions and always thank Him in advance.

♥

"For it is written, 'Worship the Lord your God, and serve him only,'" Matthew 4:10, the Bible.

11

God Requires Devotion

IN THE SPRING OF 1989 I heard clearly concerning the secular novels I had penned in the early 1980s. They had accompanied me in boxes through three moves. I was seated in my home office in our new house in Slidell when God spoke. "You have idols in your house."

"No, I don't, Jesus. I don't own any idols."

"Yes, you do."

"No, I don't."

"What about those books you wrote?"

"Oh, those . . . well, they're packed away and I have no intention of ever marketing them," I pointed out.

All of this conversation, mind you, transpired in my mind. "You need to get rid of the books," God said.

No, no, no . . . not my work, please!

From that point on, I struggled with whether I really heard from God or just felt guilty for writing them. They felt like my very own babies and I wanted to keep them locked away and safe. But, as months progressed, my guilt increased and I decided my best option was to obey God. If those novels were in any way demonically inspired, keeping them would eventually bring me grief.

So I began plotting how and when to dispose of them. The first pretty day in late spring that came along, I bundled up all four manuscripts and hauled them off to a remote building site. After cutting loose the rubber binders, hundreds of loose pages fluttered in the wind, held down by a few sticks of dry wood. I was unprepared for the emotion I would experience in destroying what took four years to create. After torching the pile of papers with a match, I began walking around the fire, weeping while watching my work burn. Along with the originals were fire-resistant copies, which seemed to take forever, hours and hours to burn.

I was determined not leave one shred of evidence behind for someone else to read. I trusted that God had purpose in what was taking place. Emotionally dismantled over what I considered a sacrificial offering, I believed this act of worship was what God wanted.

God requires obedience. With that task behind, I decided to write my testimony the following August.

While seated at my computer, I stared at the blank screen for an hour before I had the courage to construct the first sentence. I discovered detailing the intimate experiences in my life was difficult and emotionally trying. When I had finished the first draft, about a hundred pages, I told God, "Nobody will read this."

Then my home office phone rang.

"Hello," I said.

It was Joe Johnson, Jr. calling, the book editor for Broadman-Holman in Nashville, Tennessee.

"Hi, Joe," I eked a response.

"Hi," he said back. "I came across your name today while I was going through my files. Cleaning out, in fact, I'm retiring." He fell silent.

"That's good," I said. "I wish you well."

"How are you doing?" he inquired.

I said fine and wondered why he'd called.

We chatted for awhile before I inquired, "What can I do for you today?" Let's get intent out of the way.

"Remember talking to me about writing your testimony?" Joe asked.

"Yes, I enjoyed the writer's conference very much."

"Did you learn anything?"

I sensed this was one of those God-defining conversations. "The conference was helpful but I'm not a candidate for writing Sunday School lessons from an outline. I need the freedom to be more creative."

He understood. The Sunday School Board trained people to expand lessons using a proposed five-year study outline with accompanying Bible scriptures.

That wasn't me. And that wasn't why Joe called.

"Well," he said, "I was curious if you ever wrote your witness book." Blown away doesn't describe my shock. God's timing is so amazing. I had literally typed the last line to my testimony when the phone rang.

"As a matter of fact," I told Joe, "I just finished typing my Christian testimony."

"Well, I'd like to read it," he said.

Wait a minute! Didn't I just tell God that nobody would read my testimony? And now an editor wants to read it? "Well, it's not perfect, I just finished it."

"That doesn't matter. I'm an editor, remember?"

We both chuckled over his comment.

"Sure, okay. I'll make a copy and put it in the mail."

As promised, Joe read my book and it jumpstarted a long-distance friendship. A decade later, after moving to Tennessee, Joe would help me with another writing project, one that would become my most valued work.

♥

"I will have mercy on whom I will have mercy, and I will have compassion on whom I will have compassion,"
Exodus 33:19, the Bible.

12

God is Merciful

MY GRANDMOTHER CAME twice year and stayed with our family for a few months. She told me this unusual story about her older sister. Ann lived with her daughter in Memphis in a house a field away from a railroad track.

Back in the 1930s, many people travelled by bus or train. On this particular day, Sister Ann was coming home by train after visiting one of her relatives.

Ann pulled the stop cord in the passenger car, signaling for the train to stop. She got off, intent on walking across the grassy field behind her daughter's house. But Ann wasn't feeling well, and was carrying a heavy suitcase. Lord, she dreaded that walk home.

Ann tarried by the tracks as the train pulled away. About to begin her trek, she spied a young man dressed in a fine suit walking down the tracks toward her. It was hot that day, but out of curiosity Ann waited for him.

He politely greeted Ann and asked, "Where are you going?" "Oh, not far . . ." she pointed to her daughter's house. "Across that field, all I need to do is walk there."

Ann's back hurt and she could hardly catch her breath. "Why don't you let me carry your suitcase?" he offered. "You look tired, like you could use some help."

Ann said she did, and so they began walking side by side across the grassy field, the wind stirring up green grass odors seeping from the moist soil.

During their brief journey, they had a nice visit, talking about nothing in particular. When Ann stepped on the back porch and turned around to thank the young man for his help, he was gone—like he'd disappeared.

Ann's daughter opened the screen door. "Mama, come inside, it's awfully hot outdoors," she said.

"Did you see that nice young man with me?" Ann smiled at her daughter. "He carried my suitcase all the way across the field because I wasn't feeling well."

Ann stepped into the kitchen and welcomed the cooler atmosphere. "He was such a nice man."

"Mama," Ann's daughter said, "what are you talking about? No one was walking with you. I watched you get off the train and carry your suitcase all the way across the field." Six months later, Ann died from cancer.

My grandmother told me Ann's story to inspire my faith in God's ability to help people. Granny's Scripture motto came from *Philippians 4:13*, "I can do everything through Him (Jesus) who gives me strength."

With faith, nothing is impossible.

~

I can attest to the fact that one can never second-guess how God demonstrates His mercy. My middle daughter Karen was pregnant, having already lost one baby through miscarriage. Due to deliver in November, she worried about going into early labor while I was in Orlando, Florida, attending an International Aglow Conference. I assured her that wouldn't be a problem.

So I flew out to Orlando on Wednesday. Two days later, Karen's water broke and she was hospitalized. I did not receive the news until after she'd spent the night in hard labor. My husband gave me the report when I talked to him early Saturday. Karen wasn't doing well. She was in hard labor and suffering. I realized she'd been right all along. Maybe I should've stayed home.

My Aglow companions urged me to go directly to the airport and hop a flight back to New Orleans. It was still early and I needed nourishment. So I ventured down to the hotel restaurant for a healthy breakfast.

I felt in a zone of some kind, strangely unhurried. After my encounter with the saleslady at the hotel bookstore Thursday evening, I knew God was in charge and still ordering my steps. *"Be still"* came to mind.

Meanwhile, Karen was in the Slidell hospital and under duress more than I imagined. In fact, she was in danger of losing this baby. Yet, I tarried in Orlando.

While waiting for breakfast to arrive, Francis introduced me to a friend of hers from Louisiana that was gifted with spiritual discernment. After hearing about Karen's difficulty in giving birth, the friend prophesied, "Your daughter will not die, and neither will the baby." Up until that moment, I had not realized how serious my daughter's condition really was.

Now, I needed to go home ASAP.

Anxious to get to the airport and hop a flight, I hurried upstairs, hastily packed my suitcase, checked out of the hotel, and headed out the revolving front doors.

As if someone had summoned a ride for me, a van pulled up to the curb and a door slid open.

"Do you need a ride, lady?" the driver inquired

I looked at him, trusting God had arranged my transportation. I hopped inside the van and we speeded toward the Orlando airport. Introspective and prayerful, I kept silent but the driver wanted to talk.

"My wife is a Christian," he confided in me. "She's tried to get me to go to church for over a year."

This acknowledgment provided the perfect opportunity for me to bear witness of the saving grace of Jesus Christ and to encourage the man to listen to his wife. Before he dropped me off at the airport, he'd agreed to attend church with his wife the following Sunday. I paid him the fare and we parted ways.

As anticipated, the Orlando terminal was bustling with travelers. At the Delta counter I presented the attendant my ticket schedule for a Sunday afternoon flight. After explaining the family crisis unfolding at home, I asked to board the next flight to New Orleans.

The employee checked the flight schedule and noted, "There's a Delta flight leaving for New Orleans in five minutes. I'll call down and ask the pilot to hold the flight for you." So far, God had granted me favor.

After my ticket was printed, I grabbed it and raced toward the assigned gate number. The door was open and the flight attendant waved me aboard. In a little over an hour, I deplaned in New Orleans and retrieved my car from the parking lot. When I arrived at the hospital in Slidell, family members on both sides were lingering in the hallway outside Karen's room, many exhibiting red-streaked eyes from a long trying night.

"Tell me what's happened?" I inquired.

"Karen's in hard labor. She hasn't dilated, and has a 103 degree fever. The baby's heart rate is two-hundred."

I needed to talk to Karen alone.

"Honey . . ." I spoke softly, empowered by the Holy Spirit and the prophetic words spoken over Karen and my unborn granddaughter. "Do you want to have this baby naturally?" Karen nodded, tears streaming.

"Then let's pray," I said.

Together we prayed for a normal delivery, for the fever to leave, and for the baby not to be harmed. Then I stepped into the hallway and joined the other wallflowers to wait. It wasn't long before the doctor returned to check on Karen. Noting no change, she would be prepped for a Caesarian, which he would perform as soon as an operating room was available.

Forty-five minutes or so passed before the doctor came again to examine Karen. After a few minutes with her, he stepped into the hallway to update all of us concerning her condition. "I don't know what's happened," he uttered, "but Karen has dilated fully ten centimeters and is ready to give birth naturally."

Mom and Karen knew that prayer had made the difference. So my daughter gave birth to a healthy daughter in the very room where prayer prevailed.

When the nurse brought out my first granddaughter for everyone to view, all I could think about was how Mary must have felt when Jesus was placed in her loving arms. God's perfect timing. Miraculous!

♥

"In his heart a man plans his course, but the Lord determines his steps," Proverbs 16:9, the Bible.

13

God Orders Our Steps

Shirley tells this story . . .

"**I WAS TWENTY-ONE YEARS** old when I married a man mentally, emotionally, controlling, and verbally abusive. The last three years of our marriage, I hid my Bible in order to read it." Shirley's spouse despised contemporary Christian music and told her that he only wanted a "Sunday-morning" wife. She was often frightened since he threatened her on several occasions.

Fearing for her life, Shirley decided to leave her abusive husband. Taking her nine-year-old daughter with her, she left the town where she'd lived for thirty years and moved to Yazoo City where she'd grown up.

It wasn't long before Shirley met a woman who was to become her best friend. When time came to finalize her divorce, Shirley's friend accompanied her to the Pearl River County Courthouse. On their way back to Yazoo City, they stopped for breakfast then drove north on Highway 49, a familiar stretch of highway Shirley had travelled many times before. "Why am I turning right?"

Shirley looked at her friend. She didn't know, but it occurred to her that there were no turning lanes on Highway 49 between Hattiesburg and Jackson.

"You're in a turning lane," Shirley pointed out to her friend. "Just go straight." And they did.

As they crossed a set of railroad tracks, Shirley realized that Highway 49 North had no railroad crossings. She couldn't fathom how they could be on the wrong highway. Still confused over where they were, Shirley's friend kept on driving.

Soon, the four-lane became two lanes and they noticed orange cones deposited at intervals along the roadside. This signaled a construction site. Baffled and feeling lost, Shirley seriously questioned what was going on. She'd traveled that same one-hundred-mile stretch of highway between Hattiesburg and Jackson for thirty years and it had always been four lanes.

Something definitely wasn't right.

"I'm turning around," Shirley's friend decided.

The graveled parking lot where they turned around reminded Shirley of the blue-jean factory where she'd formerly worked for twenty years before getting married.

"Do you ever feel like you're in the Twilight Zone?" Shirley asked her friend, no smile materializing.

"Yeah, like right now," Shirley's friend quipped.

What had taken them five minutes or so to drive to the site where they turned around took only a matter of seconds to be positioned back at the red light where they first turned. Oddly, they were coming from the east as they spied a directional sign pointing to Yazoo City.

Two thoughts raffled through Shirley's thoughts. First a Bible scripture, Acts 8:39-40: *"I have planted your feet on a new path."* Second, Shirley recognized that God had acknowledged her situation and demonstrated that He was setting her life on a new course.

"Bring my people out of Egypt that they may serve me," God had told his servant Moses. Shirley knew now that life

for her would be different. In this confusing trek off the main road, she'd achieved peace. Healed of her unrest, Shirley realized that God was walking beside her.

No Twilight Zone accomplishes that. Shirley accepted the experience as the handprint of God on her life. Never again would she, or her friend, underestimate God's ability to demonstrate His love in unusual ways.

~

In the early 1990s, while living in Slidell, Louisiana, I attended an Aglow International Conference in Florida.

On Thursday evening, Aglow members from around the world congregated for worship at the Orlando Conference Center located downtown. After a time of singing and praising God, the speaker brought a timely message designed to help each of us define our role in spreading the Gospel. In response, our large audience clapped, rejoiced, sang praise songs, danced, laughed, cried, and prayed together. As the program concluded around 10:30 p.m., we were admonished to go out in the city streets of Orlando and witness our faith to others.

Thousands of people exited the conference center and separated. It was a pleasant evening, comfortably warm for November, so Frances and I decided to walk back to our hotel. We were hungry since we'd missed supper. Apparently, everyone else at the conference felt the same way since restaurants quickly filled to capacity.

Frances was enthusiastic and wide awake, excited about sharing the gospel message before we retired for the night. I, on the other hand, was exhausted from the long day and wanted only to locate a hole-puncher suitable for stowing my vast Aglow materials.

No happy camper, I trekked after Frances wearily on the night-lit city streets with little interest in prolonging the evening. Finally, we were seated at a restaurant and ordered our food. Gung-ho Frances witnessed to the waiter who served us. "When are you going to witness?"

I looked at my friend and said, "Probably not tonight. . ." All I wanted to do was to find a hole-puncher for my Aglow notebook and go to bed.

Back at the hotel, Frances went upstairs to our room while I made my way to the lobby bookstore. My determination to locate a hole-puncher was relentless.

I stood at the end of a long line of anxious people purchasing books and other items. When it was my turn at the cash register, the saleslady looked at me. "Are you one of those women attending the conference?" she asked after noting my Aglow nametag.

I said I was and asked if she had a hole-puncher. Then a defining moment occurred, one totally unanticipated. "Will you tell me how to be saved?"

Chills rippled down my spine. Had God sent me on a mission to locate a hole-puncher in order to encounter this lady? I asked her to step aside so we could talk.

In the next few moments, while a host of people waited in line to purchase items, I led the saleslady through a prayer of forgiveness as she acknowledged Jesus Christ as her Savior. We both cried and she returned to her post. Others in line only stared at us.

After borrowing the store's hole-puncher and punching holes in my Aglow materials, I returned to my room, never again to doubt that God orders our steps.

Jesus was busy answering someone's prayer, using me as His chosen vessel in finding this lady and telling her about God's grace through His son Jesus. As Christians, even clueless, sometimes we divinely shine.

♥

"If you make the Most High your dwelling . . . he will command his angels concerning you to guard you in all your ways," Psalm 91:9 and 11, the Bible.

14

God's Ministering Angels

GOD SENDS HIS ANGELS on earthly missions. Angelic encounters are unique to the situation, timing, and the recipient of their help. They may appear suddenly, alone, or in groups. In the Gospel of Matthew's Christmas story, we learn that shepherds abiding in fields saw an angelic host praising God and declaring that the Messiah had been born. They may assist people in dangerous situations, or observe what a person is doing.

Ray tells this story . . .

He lived with his wife in Jackson, Mississippi, and phoned my real estate office one morning. I was on phone duty and took his call. He asked if I'd assist him and his wife in finding a house. While driving around in my car looking at various properties, Ray asked if I believed in miracles. Of course, I said I did and told him one of my God-encounter stories. Then he told me his.

Ray was eighteen and in the armed service, on leave in southern California. He wasn't married at the time the event took place. Not a Christian, he was enjoying an alcoholic beverage with a good buddy at a popular Californian bar. They were partying pretty heavily.

Ray said he must have passed out during the night, because the next thing he knew he was waking up in a large barn-type metal building, gagged, tied up with ropes, and groggy. Beside him, lying on the dirt floor was his buddy, still passed out. Ray concluded that someone had slipped a sedative in their drinks at the bar.

As he struggled to get loose, he glanced around and noticed a lot of other guys were with them, tied and gagged. A narrow stream of light came through a high window, defining it was daytime. A door popped open and some Mexicans came into the building, checking their prey one by one to see if any had revived. Ray pretended he was still knocked out when nudged.

Hungry and thirsty, having lost time, Ray realized he and his buddy were in a dangerous situation. They needed to escape now. These people were thugs and meant them harm. When Ray's buddy came to, they managed to help each other get free of their restraints.

Luckily, no one was around to stop them from leaving the building. The sun was blazing hot that morning, glistening on the sandy terrain. As the two military recruits viewed the desert's expanse and distant mountain range, escaping seemed impossible.

It appeared they were in Mexico. A dusty road stretched out before them as far as the eye could see. Ray thought if they walked to the end of the road, maybe someone would stop and give them a lift into town.

About a mile down the road, Ray observed dust flying in the distance. Someone was coming in a truck and they had no place to hide. Though not accustomed to praying, he began calling out to God for help.

His buddy said it was no use. The passengers in the truck were bound to see them. They stepped to the side of the road and waited for the large lumbering vehicle to arrive. Suddenly, standing in front of them were three angelic-like beings dressed in gleaming white.

The truck rambled past Ray and his friend as if they weren't there. Then the angels were gone. Ray said they were instantly at the end of the road. With their thumbs stuck out, they flagged down a truck, rode into town, and crossed the border into the state of California.

They had been missing for a full week. Few believed their story, thinking it was an excuse to go AWOL. But Ray knew he was only alive because of the angels.

Is this story difficult to believe? Of course, it is. But as the writer, I'm telling you that God reveals Himself in awesome ways when people seek Him.

Soon after that experience, Ray went to church and accepted Christ as his Savior. He never purchased a house, and I never saw the couple again. Ray's story is a divine revelation of God's compassion.

This is Mandy's story . . .

Mandy was thirty-eight when she died from cancer in early 2014. She contracted uterine cancer three years earlier, had surgery, followed by chemotherapy. But the disease returned in a couple of years. Mandy left behind a spouse, two young boys, a sister, and other family members who loved her. Life ended way too soon.

I first encountered Mandy at our local athletic club soon after her first cancer surgery. She was vibrant, trim, and happy to be back exercising. We began our dialog in the gym's dressing room as Mandy testified of how she came to believe in Jesus. Then she shared with me her unique encounter with Jesus. . .

One night late, in extreme pain from surgery, Mandy retreated to the swing on her back porch. Alone and somewhat despondent, she began praying to God for help. Moments later, she felt Jesus holding her in His arms as He spoke comforting words. She believed that God would physically heal her after this experience.

However, sadly, the cancer returned and Mandy was told that she had less than two years to live.

Naturally, she was devastated.

I heard about Mandy's diagnosis from a neighbor and decided to visit her. Two friends from my church went with us over to Mandy's house to take a prayer shawl and pray with her. I talked to Mandy alone and learned that she was worried about leaving her two young boys behind with no mother to raise them.

At that time, Mandy's husband had moved out.

Mandy and I prayed together about the boys' futures and asked God again if He would heal her.

A few weeks later, Mandy had a checkup. I asked around at the gym if anyone knew how Mandy was doing and learned that the inoperable network of tumors in her colon were gone, but a large tumor was still lodged in her abdomen. I rejoiced, believing God had heard our prayers and Mandy would soon get better.

But she didn't. And in time, she became depressed and would not receive phone calls or visitors. At the gym, a friend of Mandy's told me that she thought Mandy was taking too many pills to counteract her pain.

I didn't know how to help other than pray.

From Mandy's own testimony, I was convinced that she was saved under God's grace and that He would never leave or forsake her. I later learned what happened to Mandy in her final days at the hospital before Hospice took over . . .

A friend of Mandy's was in the hospital room with her one evening when two male nurses arrived to tidy up the room and help Mandy dress for bed. She kept commenting to her friend how much one of the orderlies resembled the picture of her father who had died when Mandy was three. Nurse Tom even stayed behind when the other nurse left and talked to Mandy.

"Don't worry, Mandy, you're going to be fine." Tom was encouraging, reassuring her she wasn't alone.

The following morning when Mandy's friend returned to the hospital she stopped by the nurses' station to report how nice their nurses had been to Mandy, especially Nurse Tom, who had talked to Mandy and uplifted her spirits with encouraging comments.

Mandy's friend was stunned to learn that no employee by that name or description worked on the floor. Evidently, one of God's ambassadors had visited Mandy, carrying out the work of any caring angel.

It was reported that Mandy received a measure of peace after talking to Tom. Whoever he was or whatever he said to Mandy in private, people who knew her were very grateful. Mandy died a few days later.

Phyllis tells this story . . .

I was thirteen when my mother was hospitalized in New Orleans with a brain tumor. My father couldn't afford to quit his day job. As the eldest child of four siblings, I visited my mother at the hospital as often as possible. Not expected to survive the surgery, the odds against my mother were a hundred to one that she'd live through the first night following surgery, and a thousand to one that she'd recover with normal brain function.

Weeks went by as our family waited for the terrible news of Mom's impending death. Her veins were collapsing and she couldn't eat, speak, or perform normal bodily functions. Plus, she was paralyzed on one side. Several days after my mother's critical surgery, I was standing outside her hospital room late one evening and overhead a conversation between two nurses.

They were discussing Mom's condition.

"Well, we won't have to worry about her because she'll be dead tomorrow," one nurse uttered.

As a young teen, her words wounded my soul.

The next morning when I returned to the hospital, I found my mother sitting up in the bed, far from dead.

"What happened?" I asked Mom.

She looked at me but couldn't answer my question.

After ninety days, we took Mom home but she still could not speak or walk and required round-the-clock care. Six months passed and she improved. When she could speak, Mom told me about her angelic encounter.

A few nights after brain surgery, she felt a presence in her room. Someone stood at the foot of her bed. Lying perfectly still, afraid to turn over, she perceived the presence to be female since she heard the rustling of silk, like skirts. A voice told her she would not die but live to see her last grandchild born.

Mom steadily recovered, though not in perfect health as time progressed. But against all odds, she lived another twenty-five years until her youngest grandson Philip was born. She died three months later.

♥

"You have laid down precepts that are to be fully obeyed. Oh, that my ways were steadfast in obeying your decrees!" Psalm 119:4-5," the Bible.

15

God's Purposes Stand

I WAS THIRTY-FOUR years old and living in Memphis, Tennessee. Married to a Sears' executive and involved in raising three active children, I also pursued a writing career. My goal was to place my original gospel and country-western songs with a major recording artist. Like many aspiring writers, no opportunity came along.

Also involved in a city-wide Bible study that spring, I was seated at my breakfast table with my mother while working on a daily lesson that embraced the contents in Romans 9. In this passage of Scripture, the Apostle Paul is addressing his Jewish brothers in Rome. Although it was customary for the eldest son born in the Jewish lineage of Father Abraham to receive God's blessing, Paul cites an incidence when this did not occur.

This text describes God's intent for Isaac's blessing upon his unborn twin sons. Oddly, his wife Rebecca receives God's message: *The older twin will serve the younger.*

From conception, Rebecca felt the twins wrestling in her womb. Esau was born first, hairy and red. Jacob, second, his name meaning "heel-grabber" since he latched onto his older brother's foot during the birthing process. As the boys grew older, they exhibited different preferences. Jacob stayed home near his mother in the tents while Esau enjoyed hunting game in the wild.

One day, after a long hunting excursion, Esau arrived home tired and hungry. He found Jacob cooking a pot of stew over an open fire, the sumptuous aroma so enticing Esau teasingly offered to trade his birthright for a bowl of Jacob's soup. What seemed like an innocent teenage jest was foretelling of Esau's future estate.

As Isaac neared death and it was time to pronounce God's blessing on the eldest son, Rebecca arranged for Jacob to receive the blessing through trickery, trusting that was what God wanted. For me, Rebecca's ruse smacked of unfairness. Somehow, I began to associate my disappointments as a writer with Esau's stolen blessing. Maybe God was withholding my blessing while someone else received it. I know that doesn't compute.

But that was my thinking process at the time. In this raw moment of skewed speculation, by all appearances, I was indulged in a songwriter's "pity party."

But God was up to something with me. He was setting me up to receive a divine revelation. My mother listened as I read aloud from Romans 9: 15-16: *"For God said to Moses, 'I will have mercy on whom I have mercy, and I will have compassion on whom I have compassion. It does not, therefore, depend on man's desire or effort, but on God's mercy.'"*

I folded my Bible and looked at my mother.

What? The question lingered on her face.

"Don't you get it? God wasn't fair to Esau," I said. "It doesn't matter how hard I work to achieve success."

"God can do anything He wants," she reminded me.

"Maybe God won't be fair with me, either."

"But you can't know that," she countered.

"Well, I'm tired of waiting for success to find me."
Anger at the outcome of Isaac's blessing increased.

Mother didn't know how to address my comment.

"I think I'll burn all my songs (which were many), and sell my guitar and piano." I threw a temper tantrum.

She only stared at me in disbelief.

"Why should I work so hard when I have no promise of God's blessings?"

My mother was bamboozled by my attitude. She knew I'd been a Christian since embarking on my teen years. There was no question that I loved God and served in my church. My response to Romans 9 was uncharacteristic to the daughter she'd raised.

Yet, my mother knew me well enough to believe I was sincere though wrong. In the past, I had never let challenges deter me in seeking to attain a goal.

As a majorette in high school, I practiced for hours just to master one difficult twirling feat. When kidded by a male classmate about never being able to play the clarinet, I practiced days-on-end to master the instrument and sat solo chair during concert season my senior year. If anything, I'm determined and stubborn.

Mother wisely let me think about my decision.

An hour passed. My daughter Karen was depending on me to bring her science poster down to the elementary school. Still in a foul mood, I asked Mother to ride with me as I tossed a broken tape dispenser in my purse. Grabbing the car keys, we left the house.

At Brownsville Elementary, Karen's third-grade teacher, pointed me to the bulletin board at the back of the classroom. Seeing no thumbtacks, I removed the tape dispenser from my purse, noticing that its serrated edge was broken off. But it was all I had to work with.

I placed my purse on the long table situated in front of the bulletin board then attempted to tear off a piece of tape so I could put up Karen's poster. It didn't rip.

Still angry at God' unfairness in accepting Jacob over Esau, I cursed the dysfunctional tape because it didn't do what it was supposed to do. Tear and tape.

I slammed that sucker on the table, frustrated at my own limitations as a writer. To top it all, there was a young boy standing a few feet away, to my right, just watching me. Why is that kid out of his seat?

Why doesn't Mrs. Dowd tell him to sit down?

I concluded that the boy was a "dumb kid" that she permitted to roam the classroom as long as he didn't disturb others. Operating on autopilot, I picked up the tape dispenser and proceeded to tear off enough tape to put up Karen's poster. To my surprise, it ripped easily.

Upon examination, I noticed that the serrated edge was intact. Hadn't it been missing before?

This didn't make a shred of sense.

Impossible! I contemplated if I were dreaming.

Holding the tape dispenser in one hand, I slowly walked toward the exit door where my mother was waiting. She noted my troubled expression.

I opened my palm for her to view the dispenser.

"Where is your tape?"

"This is it!" I uttered.

"Oh, my Lord, He's fixed it!"

Always giving God credit . . . that was my mom.

I said nothing as we stepped into the hallway.

"God is showing you how much He cares."

No comment, the moment was too surreal.

Mother and I walked down the corridor toward the front entrance of the school. "Sue, are you listening?"

Yeah, I was. And I also realized the incident had meaning. But why did Jesus care so much? Didn't he know who I was? *Stubborn, rebellious, demanding, selfish . . .*

The adjectives were extensive.

Bottom line, I didn't deserve this encounter.

A few days later I told my husband about the incident and he said I only imagined the tape was broken. "But Mother saw the tape, too," I insisted.

Still, he didn't give my story credence.

Then I shared my miraculous story with my best friend Anita, who looked at me strangely and said, "I've never known you to lie, so I believe you."

Such a confirmation of friendship!

Two weeks passed and the incident constantly preyed on my thoughts. I needed answers. Did Mother and I both imagine the tape dispenser was broken?

Who was the boy watching me?

Did he see something I didn't?

One sunny morning, I ventured into Brownsville Elementary School again and asked the office secretary if I might have a word with Mrs. Dowd. I was sent down to her room, where I made the same request.

Mrs. Dowd assigned her students a board lesson to complete while we stepped down to the teacher's lounge.

I turned her offer of coffee down, a huge surprise to those who know me well. We sat down to talk.

Not wanting to take up a lot of Mrs. Dowd's time, I summarized what took place in her classroom a few weeks before. The deeper I got into my story, the more I noticed moisture clouding her eyes. Finally, Karen's teacher spoke. "No one was back there with you, Sue."

My gaze glued to her, I offered no comment.

"I don't even have a child by that description in my third-grade class," she explained, complicating my attempt to understand what had taken place.

We both recognized something supernatural had occurred. To say I was overwhelmed at labeling my guardian angel as "stupid" is a gross understatement.

What is God up to?

You guessed right, I did not dispose of my songs or my musical equipment. In the following decades, I continued to write in many venues: children's poetry and plays, songs, articles, and later I graduated to novels.

All this time I *knew* God cared.

I don't consider myself a highly successful writer. Not even a prolific one. But since God went to all that trouble to make a point: grace overrides ability.

Today, I am comfortable just to write.

There is no other God, no other Son than Jesus Christ, no other Holy Spirit to fill the holes of human hearts! No other God Who has the power to demonstrate His love through grace with the promise of eternal life. If I have learned anything from my personal experiences, it is that with God nothing is impossible!

Can you now glimpse the majesty and power of our Almighty Creator? What wonderful, endless plans does He have for your life? Think about it hard.

Oh, yes! Even Esau received a blessing from his earthly father, though it fell short of Jacob's anointed blessing. For through the "grabber's" lineage would be born the Messiah, the only Son of God. Jesus Christ.

♥

"He (Jesus) called his twelve disciples to him and gave them authority to drive out evil spirits and to heal every disease and sickness," Matthew 10:1, the Bible.

16

God Heals the Sick

MY GOOD FRIEND FRANCES developed a health problem. At the time, we both resided in Slidell, Louisiana, and worked as real estate agents. With no children living at home, our husbands had jobs in other Louisiana cities and were gone weekdays.

As empty nesters, we were on the verge of becoming senior citizens. Francis was no complainer. But her declining energy and discomfort in her abdomen was a clear signal that something definitely was wrong.

She'd been examined by a doctor but he offered no remedy other than laxatives to relieve the pressure.

One morning, Frances phoned me at the house and asked if I'd take her to the emergency room. My friend never would have asked if she'd been able to drive.

Recognizing Frances' distress, I set aside what I was doing at home and hurried over to her house.

Indeed, she appeared extremely ill.

"Let's pray," Frances said before we left for the ER.

Frances was admitted to the hospital and placed in a room. I spent the day with her while she waited for test results. As night fell that first evening, a young, black

71

nurse hustled into the room. We both were surprised when the nurse began praying for Frances.

We soon learned the nurse had once dated a young man involved with witchcraft. When she'd tried to break up with the Wicca leader, he'd placed a curse on her. For a whole year, she was bedridden, hardly able to walk, until God released her from the curse. Recognizing that Satan attacks Christians, the caring nurse was there to encourage Frances with prayer and testimony.

This is how Frances tells it . . .

The night before my surgery I was not in very good shape. The nurses commented to one another that my situation did not look favorable. Cold and painfully uncomfortable, the mass of gnarled tissue and fluid trapped in a transparent sack inside my intestines was worrisome. Sue Alexander and I were talking in my room when a young black nurse rushed through the door and up to my bed like she was running from a fire.

She threw her metal tray of supplies at the foot of my bed and declared in a loud voice, "You shall not die, but live to proclaim the name of the Lord!"

Sue and I just stared at the nurse in shock.

Then the nurse proceeded to tell the devil that his work was over and that I would be healed in the name of Jesus. What an entrance! The three of us talked about the nurse's prior situation with a boyfriend who practiced Wicca. Before the nurse left my room, we prayed together. She'd given me plenty to think about.

After Sue left that evening, I tried to rest but next to my bed I heard a hissing, which appeared as a writhing serpent spewing venom toward me.

I was too tired to be frightened.

I just kept on praising Christ and telling this evil thing that I did not belong to him. I quoted all the scriptures I could recall and finally slept.

Morning came and I had a final colonoscopy.

My husband, daughter Pam, Sue, and a prayer partner Joyce, were in the waiting room as I anticipated having surgery when, miraculously, the surgeon reported that the mass was no longer there.

We were anxiously waiting . . .

When the doctor came to the waiting room and motioned for Francis' husband to step into the hall, we all wondered what was going on. A few minutes later, the bewildered Lloyd stepped back inside the room and reported that Frances would not undergo surgery. In fact, she was about to be released from the hospital.

Naturally, we all rejoiced. But we also had questions regarding what happened to change the surgeon's decision. Lloyd said the doctor reported that the tumor was there yesterday, but today it wasn't.

Prayer . . . what a powerful gift to the believer!

Do I think that the doctor's diagnosis was a mistake?

No, I don't. Francis' surgeon was the person who had diagnosed my husband's cancerous polyp two years before and removed it surgically. Frances had a God-encounter, the miraculous kind! And was healed!

This is Rosa's Story . . .

I was in my late twenties. My baby was still a toddler and my husband had launched his own trucking business, traveling far too much. When he invited me to accompany him to New York on a job, I accepted.

During the trip I became mortally ill and was admitted to the emergency room in Harrisburg, Pennsylvania. The doctor on call examined me and said if I didn't have surgery I would die. I was cognitive enough to realize that would be a mistake. So my husband sent me home to Memphis on a plane.

After briefly visiting with my family, I was herded off to the local hospital. My physician was aware of my illness since I'd called ahead, but I was surprised he was there at the hospital and looking for me.

I was so sick, so out of it, I thought I must be dying. But God in His infinite wisdom and power was ever-present during my crisis. With no preliminaries, I was admitted to the hospital.

Exploratory surgery revealed my abdomen was entirely matted with infection. The surgeon installed a temporary colostomy and for several days I fought for my life. During that time, I recall hearing a nurse praying over me and felt the presence of attending angels. For the next two weeks, I was in and out of consciousness. Eventually, the colostomy was removed.

After that health crisis, my priorities completely changed. I believed in God's ability to answer prayers, and I wanted to be a righteous mother for my children and loving wife for my husband.

~

Rosa grew in statue and wisdom with Christ and became a pillar in her church. Soon, other Christians recognized that her faith was genuine. In time, she became a community leader, an advocate for the poor with fewer opportunities, and opened a clothes closet business in Memphis to meet the needs of those less fortunate. Today, she's a role model for many people.

♥

"Choose my instruction instead of silver, knowledge rather than choice gold, for wisdom is more precious than rubies, and nothing you desire can compare with her," Proverbs 8:10-11, the Bible.

17

God Honors Holy Choices

Joyce tells this story . . .

I WAS NOT A CHRISTIAN and living with a man outside of legal wedlock. Though I once attended a Presbyterian church, I had no concept of salvation through grace. I saw nothing wrong with my relationship with Jerry since many of our friends embraced our values. But all of that was about to change in a short time.

We lived on a small Gulf-of-Mexico island off the coast of Florida called Sanibel, residing in an apartment above a restaurant that we managed. Always a night owl and late sleeper, on this particular October morning, I woke up around 5:30 a.m. as I heard a male voice, gentle and deep, calling from outside the sliding glass doors.

"Ephesians 2:22," he said over and over.

I sat up on the sofa, realizing Ephesians must be a book in the Bible. With limited knowledge of the Bible, I knew about Genesis, Revelation, and the four Gospels. But what did *Ephesians 2:22* mean?

I recalled how I had travelled to Ohio the month before to attend a family reunion. While seated under a tree talking to my brother Jan, he said: "Joyce, you're living in sin and you know that's wrong." His comment hit home, so when I returned to Florida I started going to a small island church where I met a godly elderly woman named Miriam. She gave me a Bible.

Weeks passed and the biblical scripture stayed in my thoughts. It seemed impossible that someone could speak from outside my sliding glass doors since the drop to the ground from our apartment was stories high.

One night around midnight, after closing up at the restaurant, Jerry and I were in our apartment. He'd been drinking as we sat at our small kitchen table. A little tipsy, Jerry was bent on arguing and began yelling at me.

I became frightened, sensing the presence of evil. Eyes shut tight, I screamed to the top of my lungs. When I opened them again, he was spread eagle against the wall. After glaring at one another incredulously, he came off the wall and announced he was going to bed.

That was when I opened my gifted Bible to *Romans 6:11* and became convicted it was wrong to live with Jerry as an unmarried woman. Not hesitating, I grabbed my purse, contacts, Bible, and left the apartment.

For the next week, I lived with my friend Miriam. Then I became very ill. Miriam's husband, twenty years her senior with a heart condition, asked me to leave.

So I went back to the apartment.

Evening came that first night. Jerry and I were getting ready for bed. He began undressing and I suddenly felt encapsulated by an invisible bubble, unable to move. He noticed and asked, "What are you doing?"

I shook my head.

"Come to bed," he ordered.

"I can't do this anymore," I told him.

That night I slept on the sofa. During the night, I opened my Bible and strained to read the words since

I'm visually impaired without my contacts. Recalling the voice regarding *Ephesians 2:22*, I searched the biblical index to locate the New Testament book. I read these words, "For whom you also are being built together for habitation with God, through the Holy Spirit."

I read the scripture repeatedly, failing to understand it. Then I realized my brother's comment reinforced the scripture quoted by the male voice outside my window. Lying on the sofa, a still-small voice spoke to my spirit: "Joyce, when you die you will go to heaven."

Immediately, I was flooded with thoughts and memories of always wondering if I was good enough to go to heaven when I died. God knew my heart.

Jesus saved me by His grace that morning. Soon afterwards, I was baptized in the Gulf of Mexico.

I clearly recall the enormous moment of my baptism experience, the deep-rooted sense of freedom as burdens fell away and clear water rolled off of me. The truth had set me free. Jesus reached out to me through the voice, the Bible, and a friend. And I accepted His call.

~

Since Joyce is a good friend, so I know how her life unfolded years later. Jerry was saved by accepting Jesus as his Savior and they married. They lived together for several years in south Florida before moving to Dickson County where he died with a complicated lung disease.

Joyce's experiences enrich my faith as I realize we serve a compassionate God. The Bible is rich in those kinds of faith stories, incidents that happened to people from all walks of life who approached Jesus for His help.

Our Savior is vigilant in answering the petitions of believers. Are you touched by these life stories? Invite Jesus to touch your life today. You will never regret it.

♥

"In the last days, God says, I will pour out my Spirit on all people. Your sons and daughters will prophesy, your young men will see visions, your old men will dream dreams, even on my servants, both men and women," Acts 2:17-18, the Bible.

18

God Directs through Dreams

MOST PEOPLE DREAM, some more often than others. Dreams can be memorable or easily forgotten. Some are dramatic and beg for interpretation. The meaning of a dream is usually left up to the individual dreamer, though books on symbolism are available for study.

When God messages in dreams there's always purpose. Visionary messages may target a single person, specific groups of people, nations, or the entire world.

A friend of Job's named Elihu said this about dreams in Job 33:14: *"For God speaks again and again in dreams, in visions of the night when deep sleep falls on men as they lie on their beds. He opens their ears in times like that and gives them wisdom and instruction, causing them to change their minds, and keeping them from pride, and warning them of the penalties of sin, and keeping them from falling into some trap."*

From this passage we learn that godly dreams direct, instruct, forecast future events, and warn of penalties for sinful behavior. God's visual messages are purpose-driven. Whether manifested in the natural course of events, or immediately in the present, godly visions and dreams illustrate His Presence in our world and lives.

A divine revelation may confirm a decision, foretell of a danger, or simply state, "I am here and care."

One dream profoundly impacted my life . . .

The dream occurred in 1997 while I was living in Baton Rouge, Louisiana. As the scene opened, I stood in the middle of a deserted street in an established subdivision of older homes. A glint of light from the twinkling sunrise suddenly blinded my eyes. I blinked.

When I opened my eyes I noticed the houses in my neighborhood had been replaced by modern concrete condos. Baffled by the sudden alteration, failing to recognize anything familiar, I froze in my tracks.

I heard a young woman call out my name from the balcony of one of the two-story condos. "Mother, are you just going to stand there? Get the morning paper and come on up," she insisted. *Who is she?* I wondered.

I certainly wasn't going inside a residence with the presumptuous woman. But she beckoned to me again.

With no clue how I ended up in the middle of the street, I climbed the stairs to the second-story condo and went inside. Lying on the desk in the den was a real estate card, which I picked up and examined.

There were three names of owners on the card: one was Jewish, one Christian, and one Islamic. Curious, I asked the young woman why three men of so different faiths would own a real estate company together.

She replied that religious thought was blended and we were living under the religious guidelines of a world government. She told me that I was her mother.

Then, in a flash, we were at my church.

It looked different, larger with a new addition. And a peace symbol, a white dove, replaced the archaic old rugged cross that once hung behind the wooden pulpit.

"The antichrist is ruling," the woman who said she was my daughter told me. "It's how we maintain peace."

Then I woke up.

At the breakfast table the next morning, I told my husband about the unusual dream. I thought the idea was worthy as a novel theme and wondered what the future of Christianity in America would look like, ten, twenty years from now. With limited knowledge of end-time biblical prophecy, I excluded myself as the writer.

But the content of the disturbing dream stayed with me like a companion. Out of curiosity I began studying biblical prophecy with the goal of better understanding what the Bible said about the world's future. I read commentaries on the prophetic books of Daniel and Revelation. Still, I didn't attempt to write the story.

Two years passed. In 1998, we'd purchased land in Tennessee with plans to build a house and move to Tennessee. In advance of my husband retiring from his job in Baton Rouge, I listed our house for sale.

It sold in two weeks, sooner than my husband wanted to leave his job. In late December, we moved into an apartment in the city and stored most of our belongings. I had one request of the movers: don't put my recording equipment and guitar in storage. It goes to the apartment with the other marked boxes.

We unpacked the apartment boxes and my musical equipment wasn't there. So my husband and I ventured over to the storage unit to dig out my creative tools.

The designated boxes were nowhere in sight. It was evident the packers had sandwiched my "stuff" in the center of the unit and nothing would be unpacked for a full year. I was not a happy camper! No sir, no how!

"What am I going to do if I can't write music?" I fussed at my husband, thoroughly frustrated at the situation. "I specifically told the movers to take my packed equipment to the apartment. Why didn't they?"

My complaints lasted until Larry could no longer take my griping. Finally, he said his piece. "Please don't be mad! Write that book you've been talking about."

What? My husband's suggestion shocked me.

Dare I tackle Revelation and Daniel? In writing fiction, would I be able to weave a believable story within the concepts of biblical prophecy?

God, why is this happening?

After moving into our apartment in January, I was stricken with a virus that attacked my lungs. Bedridden from flu-like symptoms, bronchitis, and fever much of the time, I didn't feel like working my real estate business. Actually, I was no longer motivated to sell properties since my heart was already in Tennessee.

I lay in bed day after day, night after night, hacking and trying to get my breath. But as I lay there, I prayed about writing the dream story. Could I do it?

Soon, I began having dreams, clips of scenes as I envisioned my characters living out the story on page after page. Night after night, new ideas infused my thoughts, flooding my mind with revelation.

I crouched at our small computer in the living area and began pounding out the words in my head that described what I had visualized in dreams. Five weeks later, two-hundred typed pages, I finished the first draft.

Then we had an electric surge in our apartment.

When I logged onto my computer the next day, my manuscript wasn't there. I'd failed to back it up with a disc. It was a surreal moment. So I said to the Lord: "See, I wasn't supposed to write that story anyhow."

I decided to accept my fated loss.

A week went by and I told my friend Phyllis about losing my manuscript. "It isn't lost," she assured me. "I'll send my son over to dig it out of the hard drive."

Could someone actually do that?

Travis came over one morning, retrieved my book from the hard drive, and saved it on a small square disc.

The following August, I moved into a condo in Dickson, Tennessee. Since my husband's job had been extended for a few months, he kept the apartment in Baton Rouge and stayed there during the week. But we contracted with a builder to construct our house that fall.

With time on my hands, I reconnected with Joe Johnson, Jr., my editor friend from Nashville who had retired from Broadman-Holman in the early 1990s. When I told him about my novel, he asked to read it.

I met with Joe and his wife Mary Sue for lunch one weekday at a restaurant in Bellevue and gave him a printed copy. A month went by before I heard back from him. "This is good." He offered to edit it for me.

I originally named the book *The Christian Fugitive,* but later changed the title to *Resurrection Dawn 2014.* I knew with certainty that I never would have written this story if my creative musical tools had not been taken from me. Plus, I was too sick to work my real estate business.

What I wanted to do was taken away from me so what God purposed me to do would stand alone.

Once I'd begun writing the story, there was no stopping as the characters took on life in my mind's eye and the compelling storyline shot forward.

I self-published the first book in 2003 and the twelfth one in 2012. During those early years of intense writing, I was diagnosed with cancerous growths in both ovaries, endured chemotherapy, and contracted a nasty staph infection after my fifth chemo treatment.

Despite dealing with my health issue, I was elated at creating the series and was blessed with God's abiding Presence. The Holy Spirit was ever-present, helping me design and complete my writing assignment. I worked diligently with great joy, hurrying to finish the work.

Other dreams influenced me . . .

People were curious about how I discovered my cancer since ovarian is a "silent killer." I testify that my attention was drawn to the idea through two specific dreams. Soon after our new home was completed in north Dickson County in 2000, and we had moved in, my husband accepted a consulting job out of state.

I was home alone in the country during weekdays, sometimes traveling to Nevada to spend a couple of weeks with Larry. By that time I was outlining my second book in the Res Dawn Christian sequel.

In autumn of that year, I dreamed about talking to a former college classmate at our alma mater in Jackson, Tennessee. I hadn't seen Polly for decades. Our nocturnal visit felt very real when I woke up. Out of curiosity, I began inquiring about Polly's whereabouts.

Not until January of 2001 did I learn from an attorney friend in Memphis that Polly had died from cancer the previous fall. I was stunned by the revelation.

Was Polly sick when I dreamed about her?

It wasn't long after that when I dreamed about another friend from high school. While passing through my hometown of Bolivar in West Tennessee, I asked around and learned that my classmate had died from cancer. *Is God telling me something?* I contemplated.

Still, I did not set a doctor's appointment.

In late spring of 2001, news came that my husband's first cousin had died from cancer. I went with Larry to Manchester, Tennessee to attend his cousin's funeral.

As I glanced at the lifeless embalmed body lying in the casket, these words trekked through my mind: "You will be next." You can only imagine my shock.

This spoken word, in light of the two dreams about people in my past who had died from cancer, I questioned if some sinister illness was taking root in my own body. But like most people, I thought twice before sharing my dreams, or going to see my primary doctor.

As summer came on, I noticed my stomach had enlarged. Always possessing an hour-glass figure, with a small waistline, to have this much weight in my abdomen seemed extraordinaire. As a precaution, I set up an appointment with my primary physician.

Without examining me, he listened to my concerns then told me to come back in October for my yearly scheduled physical. Meanwhile, take laxatives and quit worrying. Gaining weight was normal for older people.

But . . . in light of my two dreams, and the words spoken to me at the family funeral, I asked Larry to feel around on my abdomen and see if he noted any lumps.

He felt something hard. So I located the phone number for a local gynecologist and called his office.

When the nurse learned about my symptoms, she immediately set up my appointment with Dr. Hawkins.

After examining me, Dr. Hawkins accompanied me to an examination room and operated the sonogram machine himself. He chuckled that he'd never used the machine, but it couldn't be all that difficult.

Sure enough, two large tumors, one on each ovary, appeared on the sonogram screen. "They need to come out," he declared. I wasn't all that surprised.

And perhaps that's why I didn't freak out. While anticipating what lay before me, surgery and pain, possibly chemotherapy, the doctor set an appointment for me with a Nashville oncologist-surgeon.

Now I needed to tell my husband.

A couple weeks later, Dr. Williams read my sonogram report and explained what needed to take place. The date of surgery was set for early September.

Waiting for my cancer surgery was grueling since no one knew if the growths had spread into my abdomen. Despite the prognosis, I clung to my faith in God.

I could be dying. But at least God has warned me.

I placed my name on our church prayer list and told friends to lift me up. During the three weeks of waiting, my stomach enlarged more and I grew a bit nervous.

The morning of my surgical event I was suffused with a magnificent supernatural peace as I felt the hundreds of prayers wash over my human spirit like doves flying up to God's throne. All would be fine.

My husband drove me some ninety miles to Baptist Hospital where I was admitted and immediately taken to surgery. While I slept, my cancers were removed.

After being placed in a room, Dr. Williams reported that the surgery was immensely successful. Everything had gone perfect, the cancers were out, but as a precaution I needed chemotherapy.

After a portacath device was installed in my left vein I began receiving the medication. Every third week, I travelled to Dr. William's office to receive the lethal chemicals that washed through my bloodstream to kill any loose cancer cells. "Taxol cocktail" it was called.

Soon after starting chemo I had what I call a "waking dream." God was speaking to me again.

Early one morning, while alone in the house, these words came: "You will be very sick but you will not die."

My goodness, I never thought I'd die!

Throughout the first five chemotherapy treatments I did remarkably well, gained weight, but was never nauseated following treatments. Of course, I endured bone and muscle aches, plus losing every square inch of hair on my body. But to feel relatively well throughout months of the medical ordeal was a huge blessing.

Then, after the fifth treatment, I developed a fever.

Five days later I was admitted to Baptist Hospital and treated for a staph infection. After seven days with no positive results from taking antibiotics, my husband requested a team of specialists in infectious diseases to evaluate my meds. More blood was drawn and analyzed.

The lead team doctor reported that I was receiving an ineffective antibiotic. The type of staphylococcus attacking my body could only be eradicated by a specific antibiotic. After receiving the correct antibiotic, my fever subsided and I was dismissed from the hospital.

I came home on Christmas Eve.

My children and grandchildren were there to welcome me. That was one Christmas I didn't have to cook. I probably looked like death-warmed-over. I expect my family thought I'd collapse at any moment.

On Monday, a Home Health representative came to my residence and brought supplies for the intravenous antibiotics my husband would administer twice a day.

What I'd heard spoken to me that morning in September proved to be correct: I was very sick but I did not die. God was not finished with me yet.

And he's isn't now. Deliverance is ongoing.

Experiencing God's divine Presence requires more than weekly church attendance. To open a channel to God's ear, we must saturate ourselves daily in His divine Word. Be still, listen, and communicate with God.

Whatever lies before, He's already seen.

♥

"But the Counselor, the Holy Spirit, whom the Father will send in my name, will teach you all things and will remind you of everything I (Jesus) have said," John 14:26, the Bible.

19

God's is Ever-Present

BEFORE THE HOLY SPIRIT indwelled the first congregation of New Testament believers on the Day of Pentecost, God either spoke in words to chosen prophets or revealed His purposes in visions. Both major and minor prophets heard messages from God that specifically impacted them or the Israelite nation.

God spoke in the Old Testament . . .

Noah, a descendant of Adam, heard from God that a flood was coming upon earth and few would survive. He built a boat according to God's instructions and entered it with his family before the earth was destroyed by water. The old world passed and the new one was birthed. Never again would water destroy the earth. To seal the promise, God set a rainbow in the sky.

Later, Abram received a call from God. He left his familiar hometown and relatives with his wife and nephew Lot to travel to a "promised land."

This land we know today as Israel.

God, being Spirit, chose common people to warn others about their need to repent of sin or suffer the consequences. Some revelations reached far into the future and have valid implications for those living today. When the nation of Judah was besieged by the Babylonians in 605 B.C. several young educated Israelis were captured and taken to Babylon to serve as slaves.

Daniel and his cohorts—Shadrach, Meshach, and Abednego—refused to cooperate with Babylonian traditions. They would not partake of the king's rich diet and insisted on a drinking water and eating vegetables.

This was a radical decision on their part.

Gaining favor from their overseer, the young Israelis were granted their choice of food and drink.

As a result, they appeared healthier than the other young men who ate the king's delicacies.

Daniel was especially blessed with knowledge and understanding of all kinds of literature and learning. As those around him recognized his ability to interpret visions and dreams, he became more valuable.

King Nebuchadnezzar had a dream he could not recall. He asked the magicians, enchanters, sorcerers, and astrologers to tell him what the dream meant.

They argued that it was impossible, since the king couldn't tell them what he'd dreamed. Furious at them, Nebuchadnezzar ordered all wise men of Babylon killed.

When Daniel heard about the decree, he prayed all night for God to reveal the king's dream to him so that he could not only save himself but all the others. In *Daniel 2:20-23*, there is a beautiful prayer acknowledging God has the power to reveal deep and hidden meanings.

During that night, the king's dream was revealed to Daniel. It was a prophetic glimpse of future kingdoms depicted as a giant statue of a man constructed of gold, bronze, iron, and a mixture of clay and iron. The final indestructible kingdom would crush all the previous others. His interpretation was true and trustworthy.

After interpreting the King's dream, Daniel was promoted as ruler over the entire Babylonian province and placed in charge of all the wise men.

Ezekiel, one of three prophets who were also priests, was a contemporary of Daniel and visualized God's throne while standing on the banks of the River Chebar near Babylon. As a "watchman" over Jerusalem, Ezekiel warned people of a coming judgment because of their disobedience and idolatry. His most famous vision has been entitled, "The Valley of Dry Bones."

This story is recorded in *Ezekiel 37:1-14*. One day, the nation of Israel would be restored, coming back together like a person rising up from the grave. Ezekiel's insight into the End Times is phenomenal as he names the nations who will organize against Israel in a final battled the Bible defines as "Armageddon."

Jeremiah was also God's prophet. His sermonic discourses were informative, instructive, exhorting, and confronted the people of Jerusalem and Judah concerning their devotion to Jehovah.

Jeremiah foretold of a coming Redeemer, an heir to the line of David, a righteous Branch who will rule wisely, doing what is just and right. He will be called "THE LORD OUR RIGHTEOUSNESS."

Jesus Christ fulfilled this prophecy and changed how people viewed God. Without the testimonies of the Old Testament prophets Christians today would have no measuring stick to compare current events.

Since Adam and Eve left the Garden, God's Word, the Bible, has been informing people how to receive the Kingdom of God, metaphorically and realistically.

Other minor prophets like Hosea, Joel, Amos, Obadiah, Jonah, Micah, Nahum, Habakkuk, Zephaniah, Haggai, Zechariah, and Malachi, had their shares of revelations. Studying the Bible opens a panorama of evidence that God is merciful, powerful, loving, and divine. He is not distant rather present at all times.

The Disciple John's End-Time message . . .

John, the youngest disciple of the Twelve, was the only one left standing after the other eleven were either crucified or murdered. His life wasn't easy as he spread the Gospel of Jesus among those living in the New Testament era. Near the end of John's life, he was banished to the Island of Patmos to live out his years.

One modern songwriter wrote these profound lyrics: *He never promised us a rose garden.* But John was faithful in serving God despite hardships. He found Patmos nearly unlivable. It was an island with rocky terrain and sparse vegetation. He lived alone in a cave, surviving on a meager diet of fish and whatever greens he could find.

But the risen Christ did not forget him. In fact, John was about to receive divine revelation and pen the most prolific book of the Bible: Revelation.

No one was there to witness how this encounter came about. All we have to go on is Scripture. John expands upon much of what Daniel said about the world's future kingdoms. Revelation is a complicated prophetic book some theologians believe is entirely symbolic while others find actual current applications.

Much of what John envisions unfolds in Heaven as Jesus the Slain Lamb reveals His eternal purposes for earth and mankind. Gleaning from John's testimony what he heard Jesus say in few statements is impossible since volumes have been written on the subject.

One fact remains valid. It's evident that God reveals Himself to those who seek Him. His love reaches out to all of humanity for all ages. Our Creator began this conversation with Adam and Eve as they walked in perfect harmony with Him in the Garden of Eden, and God continues his dialog with their offspring.

Jesus lived over two thousand years ago, fully man and fully equal with His Father. Christians trust He'll keep His word to the Twelve and return again.

When will Jesus step down on the Mount of Olives, and establish an earthly kingdom? Jesus says it's up to His Father. Only then will true peace come to earth's shores. Meanwhile, never exclude yourself from receiving a revelation from God. He's always up to something good. He's always watching with expectation.

♥

*"You will receive power when the Holy Spirit comes on you;
and you will be my witnesses in Jerusalem, and in all Judea and
Samaria, and to the ends of the earth," Acts 1:8, the Bible.*

20

God's Reveals His Will

WHEN I BECAME obedient in serving Jesus Christ as
Lord and Savior, I heard from God more clearly.

Soon after receiving forgiveness for contacting a
psychic, His Presence became more noticeable and
powerful. New gospel songs entered my thoughts and I
experienced joy again in my Christian walk.

In July of 1986 I began getting up early to read my
Bible and pray. While playing my guitar one morning, I
wrote a gospel tune entitled, "Kick off Your Shoes,
Lord." The lyrics entreated Him to come into my heart.

The following Sunday at church, Ann stood up in
front of our Sunday School class and announced, "If you
want to kick off your shoes and get involved in a
ministry, come down to the city jail next week on Friday
at 8:45 a.m." Her words brought tears to my eyes.

After the lesson ended, my husband asked what had
made me cry. I told him I believed God was calling me
to Christian jail ministry. Then I shared with Ann about
writing a song by that title, and that I'd be glad to go
with her to jail on Friday and lead the inmates in worship
songs. It was the start of a two-year mission.

Every Friday morning, I set aside my real estate
work and joined Ann in ministering to the female

inmates. They were often jailed the night before, many arrested on the city streets for drunkenness or selling or using illegal drugs. Some stayed for weeks at the city jail until their case could be heard before a judge and they were either arraigned or released on bail. Others were immediately arraigned and sent to the county prison.

During my time of serving in jail ministry I wrote many gospel songs. An inmate who had been jailed for several weeks after being charged with selling drugs offered this comment: "I need a Monday Jesus not just a Sunday one." What she meant was going to church on Sunday didn't influence her faithfulness on Monday.

I actually wrote a song by that title: *Monday Jesus*.

The ministry experience profoundly changed my perspective of the plight that faced troubled women. Not only were many materially disadvantaged, but most had not been mentored in homes with Christian values. I witnessed many inmates embrace the grace of Jesus.

One elderly lady, incarcerated for drunkenness by her own family, stayed in jail longer than usual. Ann and I commented that alcohol abuse had inhibited her thinking since she didn't seem to be in her right mind.

Eventually, the elderly woman became lucid and had this powerful testimony one Friday morning. "I just couldn't he'p myself this morning," she told everybody. "I jus' had to lay hands on Sylvia and pray for her."

"What do you mean?" Ann asked.

"I just had'ta tell Sylvia how to be saved, and she was." The smile on the inmate's face was rewarding.

Accused of a serious crime, Sylvia testified that she felt Jesus come into her heart and knew she was forgiven. Both women left the city jail soon afterwards.

Ann ran into one of the inmates we knew from jail ten years later and learned that she was still "straight" as she put it. Ann gave her copies of my gospel albums.

Change was in the wind . . .

After living in Jackson, Mississippi for nearly four years, my husband and I were established in a church and had made good friends. My real estate base of customers allowed me to earn a decent income. We were beginning to feel like Jackson was home.

During that interval of time, my eldest daughter Sharon graduated from college and moved back home. My younger daughter Karen was still earning her degree at University of Southern Mississippi, and our son Lee was about to become a senior in high school.

Just before Cecil and Deb had their God-encounter and sold their home, God forewarned me of a move.

As a broker working for a large company, I had two commercial sales contracts pending, my commission projected to be substantial. As the closing date neared, both sales collapsed on a Friday and I failed to earn $15,000 in commissions. I was burned.

On my knees in tears the following Monday, I asked God why the sales fell through. He answered me clearly:

"To make it easier for you to move."

Am I moving? I don't understand. Where to?

Wednesday evening, my husband received a suspicious phone call. After his call ended, my daughter Sharon asked, "Are you transferring, Dad?"

I remained observant and somewhat terrified.

At noon on Friday, Larry phoned me at the house and said, "We're moving." I replied, "I know."

"How could you, I just found out?"

"God told me on Monday, during my prayer time."

When I learned our new location was New Orleans, I nearly flipped out. That was the one place I'd said I'd never live. In my opinion, it was sin city.

But God had said I was moving.

I understood then why God had prepared me for the news. He knew I would resist. But going must be His will for me. Even if I had to get relicensed in a new state and rebuild my real estate business, God would never leave me alone nor forsake me. He hadn't in the past.

However, my daughter Sharon was dealing with her own crisis. A recent college graduate, she didn't want to leave Jackson, either church or her friends. But, a big *but*, she didn't yet have a permanent job or a place to live. One day she came to me and expressed her despair.

I suggested we pray over her situation.

On our knees beside my bed, we asked God together to give Sharon a job before we sold our house and moved. I suggested she contact a temporary services' agency. She applied and was thrilled with the work.

Then, a few weeks before we were scheduled to pack up and move to New Orleans, she reported good news.

"Mom, the secretary told me that a job with the company where I'm working is coming available soon."

"That's great!" I rejoiced with her. "Did you apply?"

"Yes . . ." she said, "and nobody else knows about the job since it hasn't been advertised. The secretary thinks I'll get hired." She overflowed with thanksgiving.

Sharon was hired and moved into a house with one other single woman a week before my husband and I packed up and left Jackson for Slidell, Louisiana.

I despised leaving her behind, but I trusted that God's plans for all three of my children were good.

So Larry and I moved to Louisiana in 1988. Soon after that, God revealed His plans for my three children.

One morning as I finished reading my Bible and was reclining on the den sofa praying, I heard God say, "Be still, I'm going say something."

My first response was: what in the world am I thinking? God, is this *me* making this up?

"No," the voice said, "Be still and listen. I'm only going to say this once." He had my undivided attention.

"Your son Lee will reap, while your daughter Sharon sows. And your daughter Karen will be the writer and dreamer. . ." the one-sided conversation continued for awhile, with God revealing many things about His intent for my future. When the conversation ended, I sat up on my sofa, questioning whether I'd heard correctly.

Is this something I hope for my children, or is God prophetically declaring His purposes over their lives?

Only time would tell.

This is Lee's story . . .

When God spoke to me about my son, he wasn't attending church. As a junior at LSU, Lee was walking across the campus in Baton Rouge when he noticed a student preaching Christ from a wooden pulpit beside the walkway. Embarrassed for the would-be evangelist, Lee stepped over and quietly said, "Nobody wants to hear what you have to say. You should stop."

The young man took this opportunity to witness his convictions regarding Jesus Christ and Lee came under the Holy Spirit's conviction. The following Sunday, Lee went to church with the young evangelist.

In time, Lee surrendered his life to God's will. In his decision to attend church, he met his wife. Months passed and he grew in wisdom and statue with God.

Late one Saturday, after a powerful encounter with God, Lee came home to tell his Dad and me about his decision to serve in ministry. Since then he's been intermittently involved with church-starts and Christian evangelism. Lee and his LSU roommate Stovall moved with their wives to Jacksonville, Florida in 1998 to start a church that has grown exponentially in membership.

What about my daughters?

Sharon left Jackson, Mississippi in 1990 to attend a Baptist seminary in Fort Worth, Texas. She met her husband Hal there, and today, both are involved in church-planting in the northeast. They have talented children who serve in church, too. Both recently went on a mission trip with their youth group to the Dominican Republic. Their son is interested in ministry.

No surprise, Karen keeps a written dream log and journals the revelations she receives from God. She's even co-written a devotional book of poems with illustrations that is being gifted in Florida hospitals.

Don't you love the way God works in our lives?

He was gracious to give me insight into my children's future ministries at a time when our family was going in different directions—which makes me think of what Granny Marcum told me as a child.

"I wanted to be a missionary, but couldn't because I didn't have an education." Granny said she prayed that my children would fulfill God's call when she couldn't.

Today, I am the grandmother of six, and I pray for God's hand remains firmly on these young minds as they seek out their future roles in the world. To be separated from God is risky. Stepping into the potholes of life without Jesus by Your side can prove devastating.

♥

"The world cannot accept him (Jesus), because it neither sees him nor knows him. But you know him, for he lives with you and will be in you," John 14:17, the Bible.

21

God Seeks Intimacy

THE HOLY SPIRIT EMPOWERS Christians to communicate with our Creator. Prayer is the tool. Without our Savior's leadership, we will never as individuals reach our God-ordained potential, or experience the inner peace Jesus promised His disciples.

God did not create humankind to watch from a distance as one popular song says. He seeks friendships.

And our Heavenly Father explained His plan through His Son Jesus. To jumpstart a three-year ministry on earth, Jesus chose a ragtag bunch of unlikely candidates with the goal of training them in God's ways.

Later, Jesus would equip them with a power strong enough to establish "The Kingdom of God" on earth.

Today, we know this ragtag band of believers as the Twelve Disciples. Joining a church community will encourage you in your daily walk with God and open opportunities for ministry. Studying the Bible in groups where open discussion is encouraged will help you understand Scripture. It is in this holy environment that you will learn to pray for others who are struggling just like you are in a daily walk that's sometimes difficult.

Salvation is innately personal, but community will help you move more smoothly in your Christian walk through life. If you've asked Jesus to cleanse you, join a church. Become part of God's great Kingdom on Earth.

How can we as finite humans position ourselves to know an eternal God? From personal experience, I've learned that intimacy is our choice. However, God is always present even when I've distanced myself

How can we develop a listening ear attuned to God's whispers and know when He's talking to us?

It all starts with admitting you are a sinner and asking God for His forgiveness. Prayer is a two-way conversation. Learn from hearing the divine experiences of others. Study the Old and New Testaments and discover how many who came before you related to God, and how He revealed His majesty and Presence.

Instead of becoming a reigning king over the Roman Empire as the Israelite people hoped for, Jesus chose to fulfill the role of a suffering servant. He clearly defined His purpose on earth. He had not come to judge people but to show them how to live a higher, more noble way.

In essence, Jesus undid what Adam and Eve did when they sinned. He reopened the possibility of conversing with the Almighty Creator, the ever-present, never-changing God of the universe.

Two choices loom before us: serve our own purposes or serve God's. He does not discriminate. All are welcome into His Kingdom perpetuated through grace: grace that was purchased by Jesus on the cross.

The most faithful, most devoted servant of God mentioned in the Bible sized up his position regarding holiness. Knowing he had kept the letter of the Jewish law, Job eventually recognized his human propensity for sin with the help of three devoted friends. After much dialog, Job bowed to the Creator and sought forgiveness.

It wasn't that Job had failed to obey the Ten Commandments, but rather was the offspring of people born into a fallen sinful world. To satisfy God's requirement, Job needed a supernatural alteration in his spirit. This new nature is akin to "being born again."

Jesus painted a visual picture of what grace accomplished when He ripped the veil of the Tent of Holiness from top to bottom at the moment He died on the Cross. God's throne was now approachable.

Our Creator waits patiently for each person to call on Him for help, to love Him, relate to Him, and glean wisdom. He has marvelous plans for all who are born of woman into this world. Today is the day of salvation.

The Apostle Paul summarized salvation in this way: *"The righteousness from God comes through faith in Jesus Christ to all who believe. There is no difference, for all have sinned and fall short of the glory of God, and are justified freely by His grace through the redemption that came by Jesus Christ,"* Romans 3:22-24. All are invited to join the Kingdom of God.

♥

"Let us therefore be diligent to enter that rest, lest anyone fall according to the same example of disobedience. For the word of God is living and woeful, and sharper than any two-edged sword, piercing even to the division of soul and spirit, and of joints and marrow, and is a discerner of the thoughts and intents of the heart," Hebrews 4:11-12.

About Your Author

M. SUE ALEXANDER RESIDES with her husband on a farm in Dickson County, Tennessee. Over time, she has written in many venues: gospel and country-western songs, Christian articles, children's stories and poems, and novels. She is the author of *The Resurrection Dawn 2014* twelve-book, Christian-fiction series and has independent titles listed on Amazon's Kindle site.

Visit her website at www.resdawn for more information.

Write Your Own Testimony

M. Sue Alexander

www.ingramcontent.com/pod-product-compliance
Lightning Source LLC
Chambersburg PA
CBHW062007040426
42447CB00010B/1946